AMERICAN
CORPORATE
IDENTITY 2003

Edited by
David E. Carter

American Corporate Identity 2003

First published in 2002 by HBI,
an imprint of HarperCollins Publishers
10 East 53rd Street
New York, NY 10022-5299

ISBN: 0-06-008125-2

Distributed in the U.S. and Canada by
Watson-Guptill Publications
770 Broadway
New York, NY 10003-9595
Tel: (800) 451-1741
          (732) 363-4511 in NJ, AK, HI
Fax: (732) 363-0338

Distributed throughout the rest of the world by
HarperCollins International
10 East 53rd Street
New York, NY 10022-5299
Fax: (212) 207-7654

©Copyright 2002 HBI and David E. Carter

Printed in Hong Kong by Everbest Printing Company through Four Colour Imports,
Louisville, Kentucky.

TABLE OF CONTENTS

COMPLETE CORPORATE IDENTITY PROGRAMS

SAN FRANCISCO MARRIOTT

Client
San Francisco Marriott
Design Firm
Hornall Anderson Design Works
Designers
Jack Anderson, Kathy Saito, Sonja Max,
Alan Copeland, Gretchen Cook

JOHN ZILLMER
PRESIDENT
FOOD AND SUPPORT SERVICES

ARAMARK TOWER
1101 MARKET STREET
PHILADELPHIA, PA 19107-2988
215 238 3508 Fax 215 238 3388
zillmer-john@aramark.com

Client
Aramark
Design Firm
Murphy Design
Designers
Rosemary Murphy,
Jennifer Detwiler,
Kristina McFadden

FSS500

The Core Four

1 Winning the Talent War

2 Increasing Client Retention

3 Building the Base Business

4 Selling Record Amounts of New Business

ARAMARK

PIT PASS

08447

FSS500

By winning the FSS 500, we will deliver extraordinary value to our customers and ourselves and accelerate our drive to be "the world leader in managed services."

The Core Four

1 Winning The Talent War

2 Increasing Client Retention

3 Building the Base Business

4 Selling Record Amounts of New Business

ARAMARK

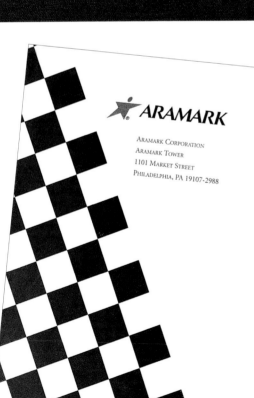

ARAMARK

ARAMARK CORPORATION
ARAMARK TOWER
1101 MARKET STREET
PHILADELPHIA, PA 19107-2988

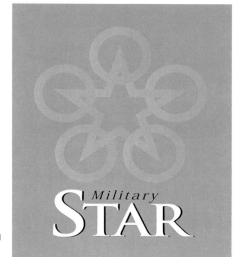

Client
Army Air Force Exchange Services
Design Firm
BrandEquity International
Designer
Joe Selame

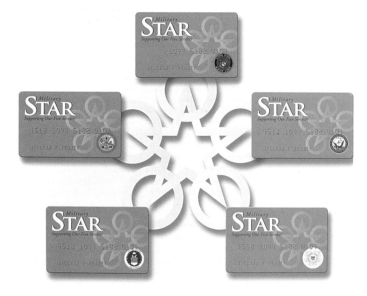

اسـتيكو
Asteco

Design Firm
FutureBrand Hypermedia
Designers
Carol Wolf, Tom Li

bromley park

crafting the patterns of a meaningful life ™

Client
The Bromley Companies, LLC
Design Firm
Noble Erickson Inc
Designers
Jackie Noble, Steven Erickson,
Robin H. Ridley

Client
Bucky
Design Firm
Hornall Anderson Design Works
Designer
Jack Anderson, Mary Hermes,
Henry Yiu, Gretchen Cook,
Elmer dela Cruz, Peggy Coats,
Cliff Chung (P.O.P. design)

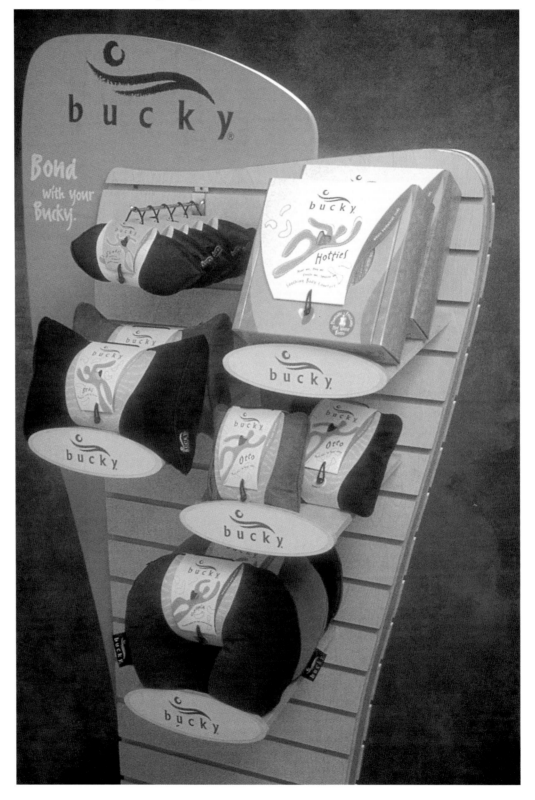

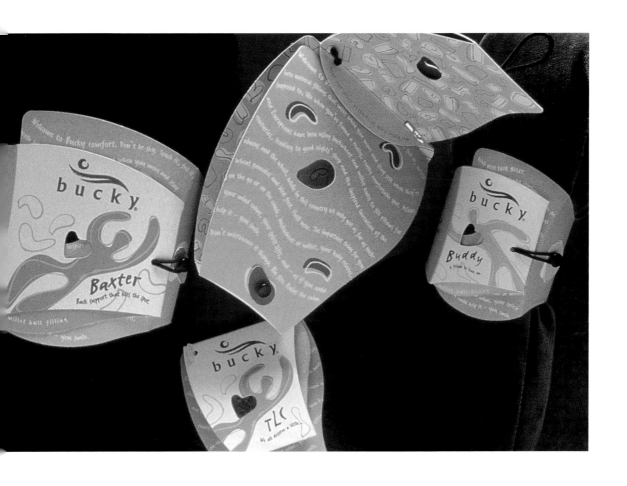

Client
  C. Shoemaker
Design Firm
  Adam, Filippo & Associates
Designers
  Martin Perez, Robert Adam

Client
Carlos O'Kelly's
Design Firm
Insight Design Communications
Designers
Sherrie Holdeman, Tracy Holdeman,
Greg Menefee, Chris Anderson

American League Charter Member

Client
Cleveland Indians
Design Firm
Herip Associates
Designers
Walter M. Herip,
John R. Menter

Client
The Coca-Cola Company
Design Firm
Jones Design Group
Designer
Katherine Staggs. Vicky Jones

COCA-COLA NORTH AMERICA PEOPLE BRAND

MENTORING

MENTORING
COCA-COLA NORTH AMERICA

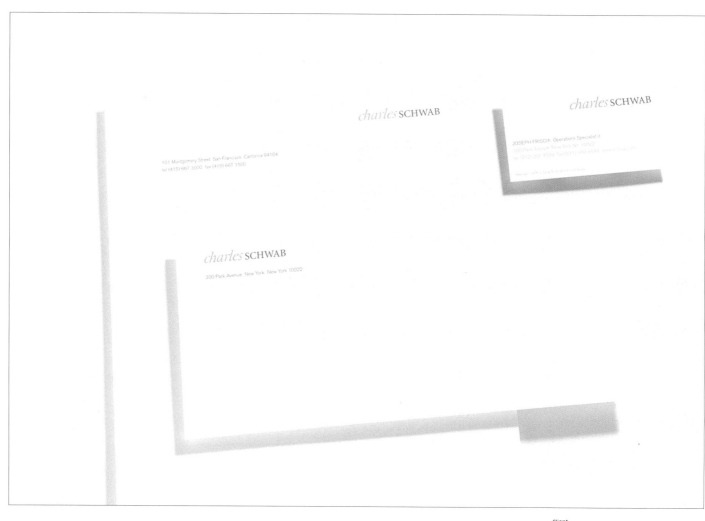

Client
   Charles Schwab
Design Firm
   Landor Associates
Designers
   Margaret Youngblood,
   Sylvain Gilliand,
   Graham Atkinson,
   Tina Schoepflin,
   Steve Holler

Client
GlaxoSmithKline/Medical Sales
Design Firm
Ideahaus®
Designers
Kevin Popovic,
Jeff Wood

Client
Greg's Body Shop
Design Firm
Bullet Communications, Inc.
Designer
Timothy Scott Kump

CARS. BOATS. TRUCKS. SPACECRAFTS.

Whatever you're driving, if it needs body work or new paint, just drop in and let us take a look at it.

There's nothing we haven't seen before so we're sure to have you up and running in no time.

And when you return home, your friends will marvel at how fabulous your new paint job looks.

In fact, they might even tell you it looks out of this world.

Painting Yesterday's, Today's, and Tomorrow's Vehicles.

Greg's Body Shop • 2419 W. Jefferson St. • Joliet, IL 60435 • 815.741.4244

RECONSTRUCTIVE SURGERY FOR YOUR LOVED ONE.

If your loved one has been in an accident – and is disfigured because of it – we can help.

We know how emotionally draining a time like this can be, but you can rest assured knowing your loved one will get the finest and most delicate care available.

We'll make your loved one look so good you'll never know what hit it.

Bringing Loved Ones Back To Life.

Greg's Body Shop • 2419 W. Jefferson St. • Joliet, IL 60435 • 815.741.4244

WE'LL MAKE YOU SEE RED.

Or black. Or blue. Or martian green or passion purple or whatever color you want your car painted.

And – we'll do it to the standards that are making us the fastest growing (*and most colorful*) body shop around.

Oh, and by the way, whatever color we paint your car you'll be tickled pink.

We'll Take Away Your Blues.

Greg's Body Shop • 2419 W. Jefferson St. • Joliet, IL 60435 • 815.741.4244

29

GROUP TRAVEL

INCORPORATED

Client
Group Travel, Inc.

Design Firm
Bullet Communications, Inc.

Designer
Timothy Scott Kump

kevin jones / partner / kevin@jobsite.com
239 fort pitt blvd / pittsburgh pa 15222 usa
toll free 1.877.2JOBSITE / fax 412.566.1256

239 fort pitt blvd / pittsburgh pa 15222 usa

Client
Jobsite.com
Design Firm
Ideahaus®
Designer
Kevin Popovic

http://www.jobsite.com / info@jobsite.com
239 fort pitt blvd / pittsburgh pa 15222 usa
toll free 1.877.2JOBSITE / fax 412.566.1256

Your boss is a jerk and you make squat.

He was *your* hire.
He's *your* problem unless *you* replace him.
Fast.

jobsite.com®

A lot of jobs. A lot of people looking for jobs.™

And a big ol' website that helps them find each other. Jobs in construction, real estate, real estate finance and related industries. And people already in the business looking to make a change.

What else could you want?

Okay, you can also post resumes, jobs and company profiles. Monitor the traffic on resumes, profiles or jobs. Search jobsite.com's database to match the right person to the right job. Even get news, tips and tricks from industry pros.

Stop by and see for yourself. If you have any questions drop us a line at info@jobsite.com, or call toll free 1-877-2JOBSITE.

See ya there.

Client
  Landshire, Inc.
Design Firm
  Dixon & Parcels Associates, Inc.
Designers
  Dixon & Parcels Associates, Inc.

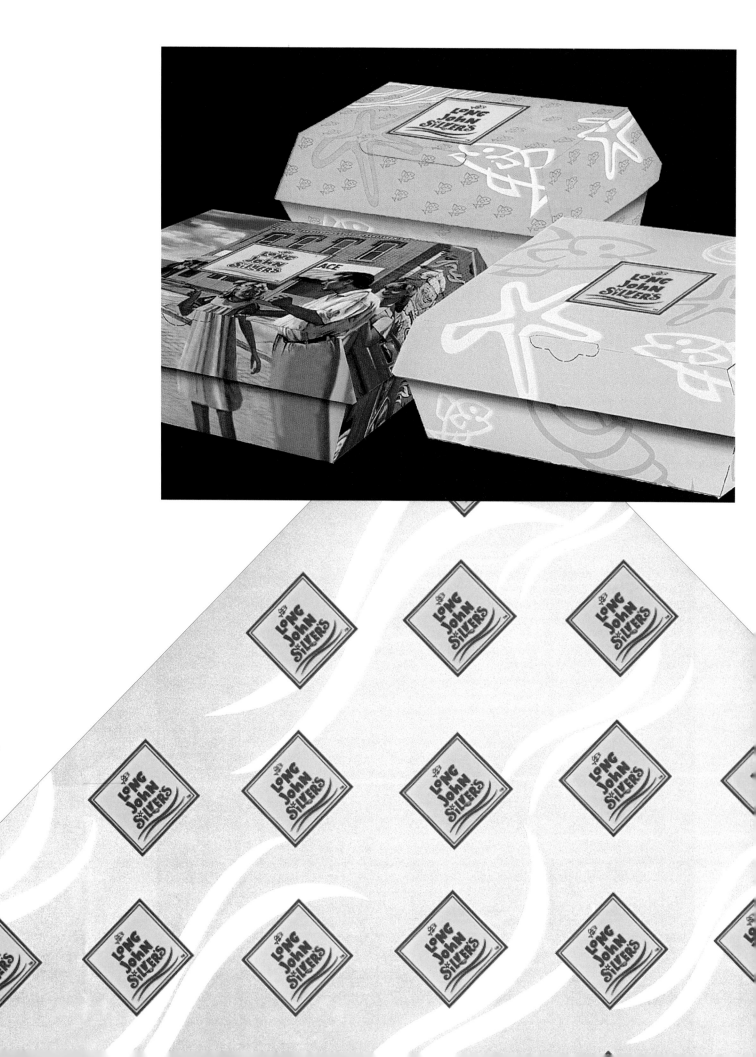

Client
 Long John Silver's
Design Firm
 King Casey
Designers
 John Chrzanowski,
 Steve Brent,
 Carolina Guimarey

Client
Mars Music
Design Firm
BrandEquity International
Designer
Joe Selame

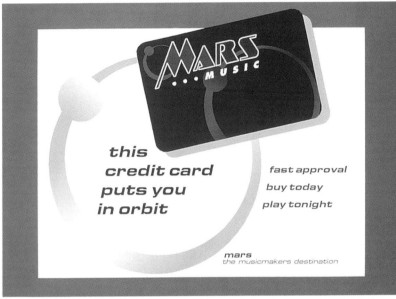

this
credit card
puts you
in orbit

fast approval
buy today
play tonight

mars
the musicmakers destination

Media Loft

Client
Media Loft
Design Firm
Larsen Design + Interactive
Designer
Bill Pflipsen

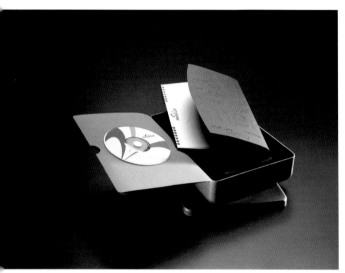

POLYVISION

Client
 PolyVision Corporation
Design Firm
 Jones Design Group
Designers
 Katherine Staggs, Vicky Jones

Client
Miami Valley Black Pages
Design Firm
Anise V. Simpson
Graphic Designer/Illustrator
Designer
Anise V. Simpson

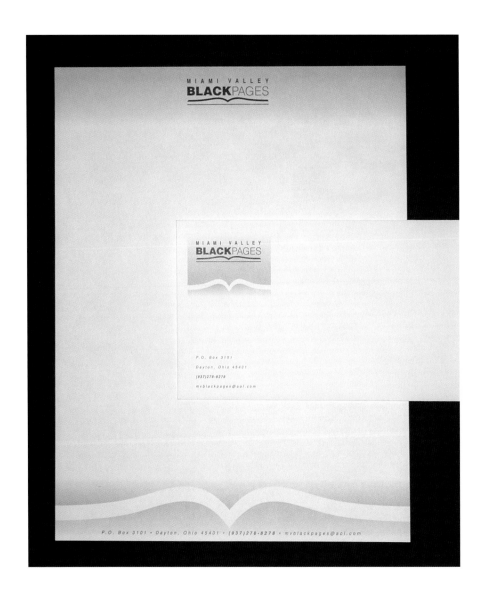

(continued)
Client
Miami Valley Black Pages
Design Firm
**Anise V. Simpson
Graphic Designer/Illustrator**

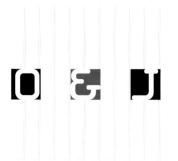

Design, Inc.

Client
O & J Design, Inc.
Design Firm
O & J Design, Inc.
Designer
Andrzej Olejniczak

nexen™

Client
Nexen
Design Firm
Larsen Design + Interactive
Designer
Bill Plipsen

World Access

Client
World Access

Design Firm
Jones Design Group

Designer
Vicky Jones

Client
O-Company
Design Firm
BrandEquity International
Designer
Joe Selame

Client
One World
Design Firm
Hornall Anderson Design Works
Designers
Jack Anderson, John Anicker, Andrew Smith,
Andrew Wicklund, Mary Hermes, John Anderle

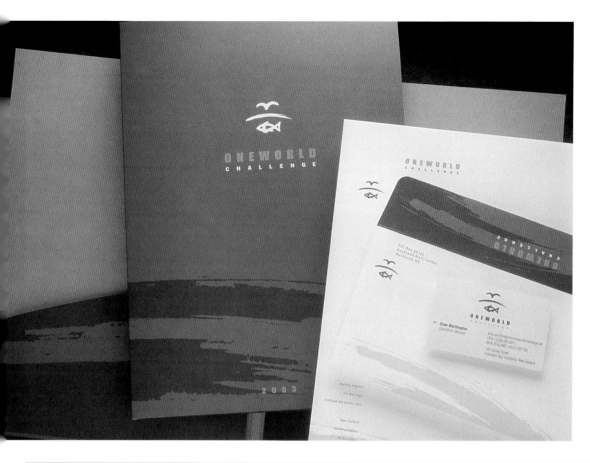

Client
Sony Computer Entertainment America
Design Firm
Creative Dynamics, Inc.
Designers
Eddie Roberts, Victor Rodriguez,
Chris Smith, Mackenzie Walsh,
Casey Corcoran

O

ORRICK

Client
Orrick Herrington & Sutcliffe
Design Firm
Greenfield/Belser
Designer
Stephanie Fernandez

ORRICK

ORRICK

LONDON LOS ANGELES NEW YORK SACRAMENTO SAN FRANCISCO
SEATTLE SILICON VALLEY SINGAPORE TOKYO WASHINGTON DC

RALPH BAXTER
chairman & chief executive officer

ORRICK, HERRINGTON & SUTCLIFFE LLP
666 FIFTH AVENUE
NEW YORK, NY 10103-0001

tel 212-506-5000
fax 212-506-5151
ralphbaxter@orrick.com

WWW.ORRICK.COM

ORRICK

ORRICK, HERRINGTON & SUTCLIFFE LLP

HIGHLIGHTS

O

ORRICK

o-*benefits*

FAST FUTURE

"Few firms have made their mark as Orrick has"
(vault.com)

"fierce competitor that knows how to stay on top"
(California Law Business)

"exciting clients, challenging work and fulfilling
environment" *(vault.com)*

ORRICK

SUMMERTIME

An "outstanding....excellent" summer program
(information.com)

"the most non-cynical place" *(American Lawyer)*

"an informal and fun place to work" *(information.com)*

ORRICK

To learn more about the firm people are
talking about, visit www.orrick.com or call
Francesca Runge at 212-506-3556 or Marty
Martinez at 415-773-5599.

ORRICK

NO SPIN

ORRICK

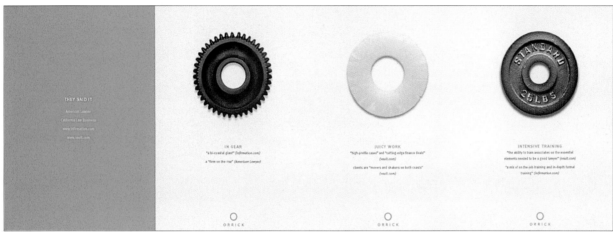

THEY SAID IT

American Lawyer
California Law Business
www.information.com
www.vault.com

IN GEAR

"a bi-coastal giant" *(information.com)*

a "firm on the rise" *(American Lawyer)*

ORRICK

JUICY WORK

"high-profile cases" and "cutting-edge finance deals"
(vault.com)

clients are "movers and shakers on both coasts"
(vault.com)

ORRICK

INTENSIVE TRAINING

"the ability to train associates on the essential
elements needed to be a good lawyer" *(vault.com)*

"a mix of on-the-job training and in-depth formal
training" *(information.com)*

ORRICK

(continued)
Client
 Orrick Herrington & Sutcliffe
Design Firm
 Greenfield/Belser

ORRICK
GLOBAL LAWYERS

Meridian
INTERNATIONAL CENTER

The Meridian

Meridian International
Center Newsletter
Winter 2001–2002

Exchange

INSIDE

3 Ball Raises Funds
Over 750 guests attended the thirty-third annual Meridian Ball, which raised more than $400,000 in support of Meridian's efforts to promote international understanding.

4 Secretary Powell Meets with Journalists
A delegation of Central Asian journalists met with Secretary of State Colin Powell during a recent Meridian program.

6 Senators Mitchell and Rudman Explore Peace Prospects
George Mitchell and Warren Rudman spoke at Meridian about prospects for ending Israeli-Palestinian violence.

9 New Exhibition Will Celebrate American Spirit
Meridian is organizing True Colors: Meditations on the American Spirit, a response by artists to the events of September 11.

11 Linden Circle Offers New Programs
Meridian's newly named Linden Circle welcomes young professionals interested in international affairs.

SEPTEMBER 11: THE GLOBAL AFTERMATH

Meridian conducted two special series of seminars this Fall to provide a better understanding of what lies beneath the tragic events of September 11. The speakers discussed the causes and historical events that led up to the attacks, and also provided insights into the impacts in the United States and abroad.

The initial seminar on *Islam, Justice, and War* featured **Aly Abuzaakouk**, Executive Director of the American Muslim Council, and **Maysan Al-Faruqi**, Assistant Professor of Islamic Studies at Georgetown University. **Richard Murphy, Robert Pelletreau, Robin**

(Continued on page 2)

Lucius Battle (far left) is joined by other former assistant secretaries of state (left-right) Nicholas Veliotes, Robert Pelletreau, Robin Raphel, and Edward Walker, together with Meridian President Walter Cutler following a seminar on regional ramifications of the September 11 attacks.

JAMES JONES ELECTED NEW CHAIRMAN

James R. Jones

Meridian's trustees have elected The Honorable **James R. Jones** as chairman of the board. Ambassador Jones, who has been a member of Meridian's Board of Trustees for the past year, begins his new position on January 1. He will succeed **Colleen Nunn**, who is completing her two-year term as chairman.

Ambassador Jones is chief executive officer of Manatt Jones Global Strategies. He previously served as U.S. ambassador to Mexico from 1993 to1997, where he played a key role during the Mexican peso crisis, the passage and implementation of NAFTA, and in developing new, cooperative efforts to combat drug trafficking.

Ambassador Jones also served as president at Warnaco International; as chairman and CEO of the American Stock Exchange from 1989 to 1993; and as a member of the U.S. House of Representatives from Oklahoma from 1973 to 1987. In Congress, he was chairman of the House Budget Committee and a ranking member of the House Ways and Means Committee. He also served as appointments secretary (now called chief of staff) to President Lyndon Johnson.

Ambassador Jones serves as a director for Anheuser Busch, Keyspan Energy Corporation, Kansas City Southern Industries, the American Red Cross, the Kaiser Family Foundation, and the U.S.-Mexico Business Commission. He is a graduate of the University of Oklahoma and Georgetown University Law Center.

Client
Meridian International Center
Design Firm
TGD Communications, Inc.
Designers
Rochelle Gray, Gloria Vestal

Arts
Programs

PRESENTING
ART AND
CULTURE FROM
AROUND
THE WORLD

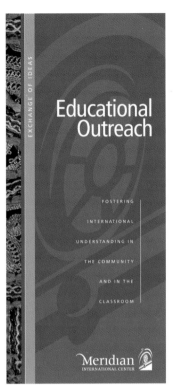

Educational
Outreach

FOSTERING
INTERNATIONAL
UNDERSTANDING IN
THE COMMUNITY
AND IN THE
CLASSROOM

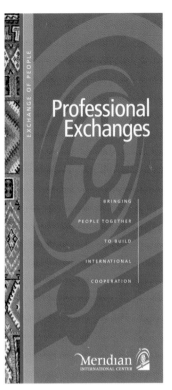

Professional
Exchanges

BRINGING
PEOPLE TOGETHER
TO BUILD
INTERNATIONAL
COOPERATION

Client
Restaurant Brokers
Design Firm
Jones Design Group
Designer
Vicky Jones

WWW.RESTAURANT-BROKERS.COM

THE BUSINESS OF RESTAURANTS™

www.restaurant-brokers.com

Client
    Seattle Sonics
Design Firm
    Hornall Anderson Design Works
Designers
    Jack Anderson, Mary Popich,
    Andrew Wicklund, Elmer dela Cruz

Client
Palm Island Developers
Design Firm
FutureBrand
Designers
Carol Wolf, Thomas Nguy, Tom Li

(continued)
Client
  Palm Island Developers
Design Firm
  FutureBrand

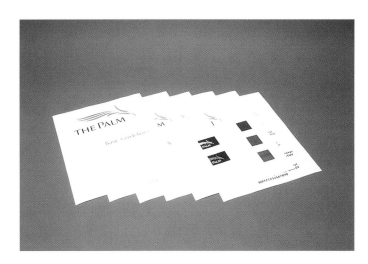

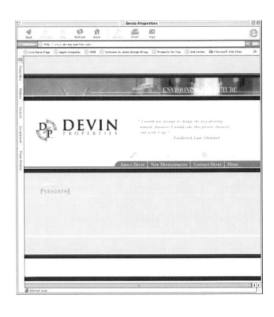

Client
  Devin Properties
Design Firm
  Jones Design Group
Designer
  Katherine Staggs, Vicky Jones

PACKAGE DESIGNS

Client
   Seafarer Baking Co.
Design Firm
   Sabingrafik, Inc.
Designer
   Tracy Sabin

Client
   Laurel Glen
Design Firm
   Buttitta Design
Designers
   Lisa Ray Hobro, Patti Buttitta

Client
   Frito Lay
Design Firm
   Landor Associates
Designer
   Jonathan Weden, Jeanne Reimer

Client
   Michaels
Design Firm
   Design Resource Center
Designer
   John Norman

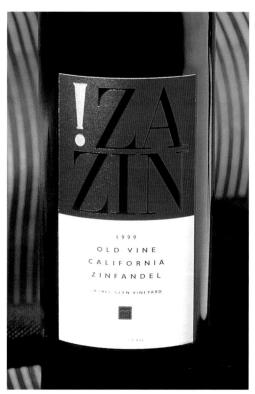

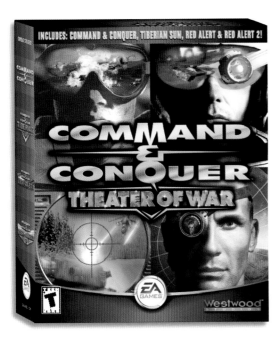

Client
  Westwood Studios
Design Firm
  Creative Dynamics, Inc.
Designers
  Eddie Roberts, Victoria Hart

Client
  LifeSavers
Design Firm
  LMS Design, Inc.
Designers
  Richard Shear, Alex Williams

Client
  Bennie Factor Products
Design Firm
  Route 8, A Design Firm
Art Director
  Janet Rauscher
Designer
  Russ Jackson

Client
  Clearly Canadian Beverage Corporation
Design Firm
  Karacters Design Group
Creative Director
  Maria Kennedy
Associate Creative Director
  Matthew Clark

Client
  Trefethen Vineyards
Design Firm
  Design Solutions
Designer
  Deborah Mitchell

Client
  Swither
Design Firm
  Phillips Design Group
Designer
  Alison Goudreault

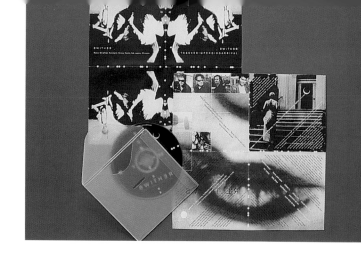

Client
  Trefethen Vineyards
Design Firm
  Design Solutions
Designer
  Deborah Mitchell

Client
  Frederick
  Wildman & Sons
Design Firm
  **Buttitta
  Design**
Designer
  Patti Buttitta
Illustrator
  Lori Almeida

Client
  Adrienne's Gourmet Food
Design Firm
  Mark Oliver, Inc.
Designers
  Mark Oliver, Patty Driskel

Client
Hain/Celestial Food Group
Design Firm
Mark Oliver, Inc.
Designers
Mark Oliver, Patty Driskel

Client
Predictive Systems
Design Firm
Cullinane Design
Designer
Jean Kim

Client
Lindt Chocolate
Design Firm
Millyard Design Assoc. Ltd.
Designers
Marjorie Millyard, Paula Cavallaro

Client
Landmark Vineyards
Design Firm
Buttitta Design
Designer
Patti Buttitta

Client
  Big Bark Bakery
Design Firm
  Kendall Creative Shop
Designers
  Tim Childress, Mark K. Platt,
  Jennifer Brehm

Client
  Betty Crocker
Design Firm
  Compass Design
Designers
  Mitch Lindgren, Bill Collins,
  Tom Arthur, Rich McGowen

Client
  Jetmax International
Design Firm
  Design Resource Center
Designer
  John Norman

Client
  Big Bark Bakery
Design Firm
  Kendall Creative Shop
Designers
  Tim Childress, Mark K. Platt

Client
The Bachman Company
Design Firm
Dixon & Parcels Associates, Inc.
Designers
Dixon & Parcels Associates, Inc.

Client
Hershey Foods Corporation
Design Firm
Dixon & Parcels Associates, Inc.
Designers
Dixon & Parcels Associates, Inc.

Client
Daddy Sam's
Design Firm
Compass Design
Designers
Mitch Lindgren, Tom Arthur,
Bill Collins

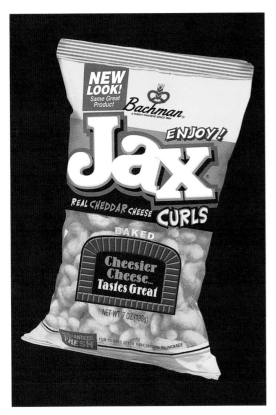

Client
Essential Skin
Design Firm
Allen Bell Spencer
Designer
Allen Weideman
Photographer
Elde Stewart

Client
Florida's Natural Growers
Design Firm
Dixon & Parcels Associates, Inc.
Designers
Dixon & Parcels Associates, Inc.

Client
Kemps
Design Firm
Compass Design
Designers
Mitch Lindgren, Rich McGowen

Client
Amazing Planes
Design Firm
Red Herring Design
Designer
Matt Bouloutian

Client
Crystal Farms
Design Firm
Compass Design
Designers
Mitch Lindgren, Bill Collins,
Tom Arthur, Rich McGowen

Client
  BC–USA
Design Firm
  LMS Design, Inc.
Designer
  Richard Shear

Client
  GE/Sanyo
Design Firm
  Zen Design Group
Designer
  Kok Hwa Chung

Client
  Coleman Company
Design Firm
  Landor Associates
Designers
  Nicolas Aparicio, Christopher Lehmann, Anastasia Laksmi

Client
  Bayer Corporation Consumer Care
Design Firm
  Szylinski Associates Inc.
Designer
  Ed Szylinski

Client
Unilever
Design Firm
R.BIRD
Designer
Joseph Favata

Client
Unilever
Design Firm
R.BIRD
Designers
Joseph Favata, Michele Li

Client
Worldwide Medical
Design Firm
Vince Rini Design
Designer
Vince Rini

Client
Chandon Estates
Design Firm
Landor Associates
Designers
John Kiil, Nicolas Aparicio,
Christopher Lehmann

Client
Bayer Corporation Consumer Care
Design Firm
Szylinski Associates Inc.
Designer
Ed Szylinski

Client
Sara Lee Bakery
Design Firm
Haugaard Creative Group
Designers
Tony Cesare, Erin Kennedy

Client
Coleman Company
Design Firm
Landor Associates
Designers
Nicolas Aparicio, Christopher Lehmann,
Sean McGrath, Philip Foster

Client
Unilever
Design Firm
R.BIRD
Designer
Joseph Favata

Client
Bestfoods
Design Firm
R.BIRD
Designers
Joseph Favata, Michele Li

Client
All Glass Aquarium
Design Firm
Design North
Designer
Mark Topczewski

Client
Lipton
Design Firm
R.BIRD
Designers
Joseph Favata, Kelly Behan

Client
Wine Design
Design Firm
Brand, Ltd.
Designers
Scott Wizell, Virginia Thompson Martino

Client
Paramount Home Video
Design Firm
30sixty Design
Art Director
Par Larsson
Designer
Ethan Archer

Client
Benevolence
Design Firm
Brand, Ltd.
Designers
Virginia Thompson Martino,
Yuroz, Mark Martino

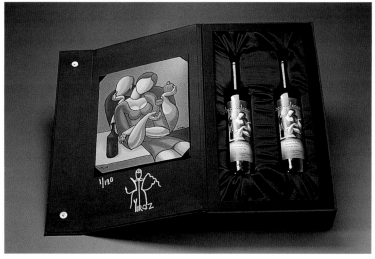

Client
Benevolence
Design Firm
Brand, Ltd.
Designers
Virginia Thompson Martino,
Mark Martino, Yuroz

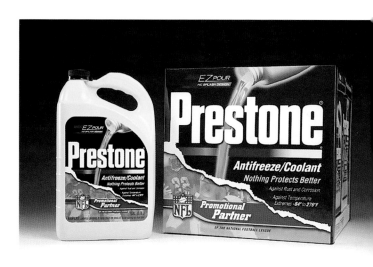

Client
Honeywell Consumer Products Group
Design Firm
Tom Fowler, Inc.
Designers
Mary Ellen Butkus, Paul Beichert

Client
    Koch Foods, Inc.
Design Firm
    Design Resource Center
Designer
    John Norman

Client
    D & D Commodities Ltd.
Design Firm
    MVP Marketing & Design Inc.
Designers
    Alex Watkins, Greg Schultz

Client
    Usana
Design Firm
    Landor Associates
Designers
    Nicolas Aparicio, Anastasia Laksmi

Client
    Johnson & Johnson Consumer Products Co.
Design Firm
    LMS Design, Inc.
Designers
    Pam Shear, Alex Williams

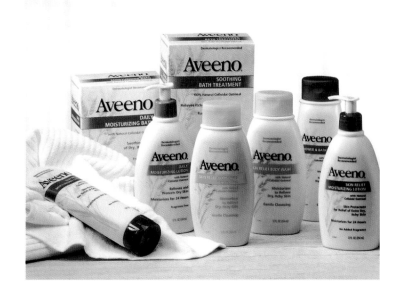

Client
    Citrus World, Inc.
Design Firm
    Dixon & Parcels Associates, Inc.
Designers
    Dixon & Parcels Associates, Inc.

Client
    Rand McNally
Design Firm
    Landor Associates
Designers
    Nicolas Aparicio, Anne Asche

Client
    Playtex Products, Inc.
Design Firm
    Zunda Design Group
Designers
    Todd Nickel, Charles Zunda,
    Paul LaPlaca

Client
    Tommyco
Design Firm
    Compass Design
Designer
    Bill Collins, Rich McGowen

Client
Rocky Mountain Chocolate Factory
Design Firm
Hornall Anderson Design Works
Designers
Larry Anderson, Jack Anderson,
Gretchen Cook, Jay Hilburn,
Kaye Farmer, Andrew Wicklund

Client
Robinson Knife Company
Design Firm
Michael Orr & Associates, Inc.
Designers
Michael R. Orr, Thomas Freeland

Client
People Gotta Eat
Design Firm
Kendall Creative Shop
Designer
Mark K. Platt

Client
Bee International
Design Firm
Sabingrafik, Inc.
Designer
Tracy Sabin

Client
  General Mills
Design Firm
  Lipson Alport Glass & Associates
Designer
  Lori Cerwin

Client
  Maryhill Winery
Design Firm
  Klündt Hosmer Design
Designers
  Darin Klündt, Judy Heggem-Davis

Client
  Tamansari Beverage
Design Firm
  Sabingrafik, Inc.
Designers
  Tracy Sabin, Karim Amiryani

Client
  NexPress
Design Firm
  Forward branding & identity

Client
  Encore
Design Firm
  DuPuis
Designers
  Jack Halpern, John Silva,
  Mario Soto

Client
  Acco Brands
Design Firm
  DuPuis
Designers
  Steven DuPuis, Jack Halpern,
  Heesyun Ruetgers, Bill Peirce,
  Tim Schmidt

Client
  Encore
Design Firm
  DuPuis
Designers
  Jack Halpern, John Silva,
  Mario Soto

Client
  The Coca-Cola Company
Design Firm
  Lipson Alport Glass & Assoc.
Designers
  Lori Cerwin, Jon Shapiro, Eric Timm

Client
   Cape Shore
Design Firm
   Cape Shore
Designers
   Lynnea Washburn, Melody Martin

Client
   Epos Concepts, Inc.
Design Firm
   Epos, Inc.
Art Director
   Gabrielle Raumberger
Designers
   Eric Martinez, Clifford Singontiko

Client
   Ocean Spray
Design Firm
   LMS Design, Inc.
Designers
   Richard Shear, Rick Mapes

Client
   Epos Concepts, Inc.
Art Director
   Gabrielle Raumberger
Designer
   Clifford Singontiko

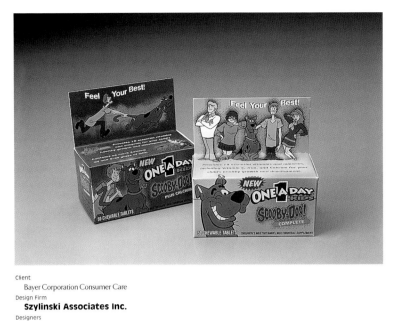

Client
    Epos Concepts, Inc.
Design Firm
    Epos, Inc.
Creative Director
    Gabrielle Raumberger
Designer
    Clifford Singontiko

Client
    Bayer Corporation Consumer Care
Design Firm
    Szylinski Associates Inc.
Designers
    Ed Szylinski, Frank Castaldi

Client
    Bayer Corporation Consumer Care
Design Firm
    Szylinski Associates Inc.
Designers
    Ed Szylinski, Frank Castaldi

Client
    Kemps
Design Firm
    Compass Design
Designers
    Mitch Lindgren, Rich McGowen

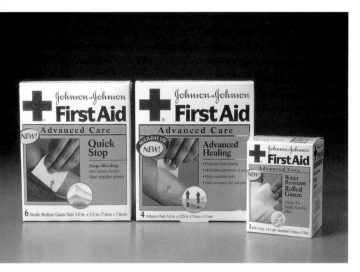

Client
Johnson & Johnson Consumer Products
Design Firm
Szylinski Associates/Protocol
Designers
Ed Szylinski, Joe Gregory,
John Lyons, Steven Shirack

Client
Allied Domecq
Design Firm
Landor Associates
Designers
Nicolas Aparicio, Laura Kuhn,
Philip Foster

Client
Corn Poppers
Design Firm
Axion Design Inc.

Client
Tootsie Roll Industries
Design Firm
Cassata & Associates
Designers
Lesley Wexler, James Wolfe

Client
High Falls Brewing Company
Design Firm
McElveney & Palozzi Design Group
Designers
Jon Westfall, Nick Woyciesjes.
Mike Johnson

Client
Morey's Seafood International
Design Firm
Mackey Szar

Client
Target Corporation
Design Firm
Target Advertising
Designer
Angela Johansen

Client
CNS
Design Firm
Mackey Szar

Client
    Miller Brewing Company
Design Firm
    Design Partners Incorporated
Designer
    Mike Oberheu

Client
    Target Corporation
Design Firm
    Target Advertising
Designer
    Angela Johansen

Client
    Miller Brewing Company
Design Firm
    Design Partners Incorporated
Designer
    Barbara Hannagan

Client
    Target Corporation
Design Firm
    Target Advertising
Designer
    Sara Johnson

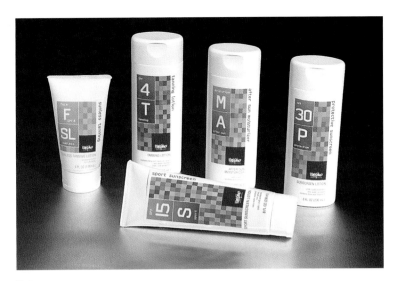

Client
  Target Corporation
Design Firm
  Design Guys
Art Director
  Steve Sikora
Designer
  Anne Peterson

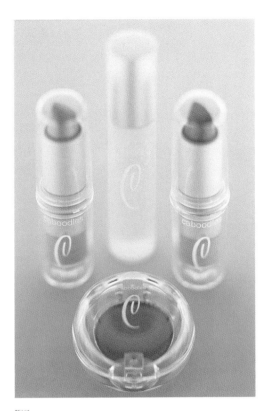

Client
  Caboodles Cosmetics
Design Firm
  Karacters Design Group
Creative Director
  Maria Kennedy
Designer
  Michelle Melenchuk

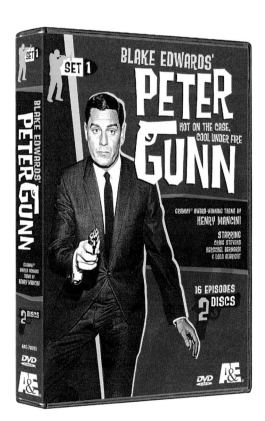

Client
  A&E
Design Firm
  The Sloan Group
Designer
  Sandra Nevistich

Client
  Friskies Pet Care Co., Inc.
Design Firm
  Thompson Design
Designers
  Patrick Fraser, Elizabeth Berth

Client
Nestlé USA
Confections & Snacks Div.
Design Firm
Thompson Design
Designer
Trevor Thompson

Client
C*me Cosmetics
Design Firm
Karacters Design Group
Creative Director
Maria Kennedy
Designer
Michelle Melenchuk

Client
Tin Woodsman
Design Firm
Poppie Advertising Design, Inc.
Designer
Erika Carvalho

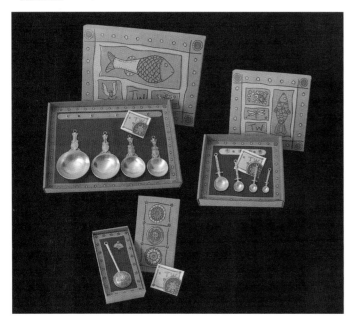

Client
Master Lock Company
Design Firm
Design Partners Incorporated
Designer
Tom Gawle

Client
  IQ Hong Kong
Design Firm
  Zen Design Group
Designer
  David Perrin

Client
  Kraft Foods Incorporated
Design Firm
  Design Partners Incorporated
Designers
  Barbara Hannagan, Craig Stodola

Client
  GE/Sanyo
Design Firm
  Zen Design Group
Designer
  Matt Chapman

Client
  Johnson Outdoors
Design Firm
  Design Partners Incorporated
Designer
  Tom Gawle

Client
    Wallace Church, Inc.
Design Firm
    Wallace Church, Inc.
Designers
    Jeremy Creighton, Stan Church

Client
    Eastman Kodak Company
Design Firm
    Forward branding & identity

Client
    Wegmans Food Markets, Inc.
Design Firm
    Forward branding & identity

Client
    The Catering Company
Design Firm
    Red Canoe
Art Director
    Deb Koch
Designer
    Caroline Kavanagh
Illustrator
    Diana Huff

Client
Shaw's
Design Firm
C&M Marketing
Art Director
David Gurman
Designer
Jeff Powers
Photography
Jens Johnson

Client
Heinz
Design Firm
**Lipson Alport Glass & Assoc.
Cincinnati Office**
Design Director
Scott Smith
Designer
Sharon Mirande

Client
Kodak
Design Firm
Wallace Church, Inc.
Designers
Lawrence Haggerty, Stan Church

Client
San-J International
Design Firm
Gauger & Silva
Designer
Lori Murphy

Client
Robinson Knife Company
Design Firm
Michael Orr + Associates, Inc.
Designers
Michael R. Orr, Thomas Freeland

Client
Microsoft
Design Firm
Landor Associates/Seattle
Designers
Jeremy Dawkins, Kenny Chui

Client
Heinz Pet Foods
Design Firm
Design North
Design Director
L. Patrick Cowen

Client
Agrilink Foods/Birdseye
Design Firm
Design North
Creative Director
Gwen Granzow

Client
Iceland Spring
Design Firm
The Sloan Group
Designer
Sean Mosher-Smith

Client
Mead School and Office Products
Design Firm
Brady Communications
Designers
John Brady, Rick Madison,
Kevin Kennedy

Client
NYFIX
Design Firm
Cullinane Design
Designer
Jenn Perman

Client
Galaxy Desserts
Design Firm
Gauger & Silva
Designer
Isabelle Laporte

Client
Unilever
Design Firm
Wallace Church, Inc.
Designers
John Bruno ,Thorny Church, Stan Church

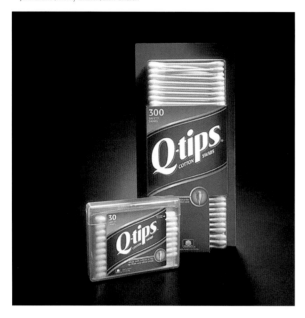

Client
Petsmart
Design Firm
C&M Marketing
Art Director
David Gurman
Designer, Illustrator
Jane Atwell

Client
Petsmart
Design Firm
C&M Marketing
Designers
Jeff Powers, Sue Sottile, David Gurman

Client
Snapple Beverage Group
Design Firm
HMS Design
Designer
Marjon LeQuesne

Client
Weis
Design Firm
C&M Marketing
Art Director
David Gurman
Designer
Jeff Powers

Client
PNY Technologies, Inc.
Design Firm
CAG Design
Designer
David Motyl

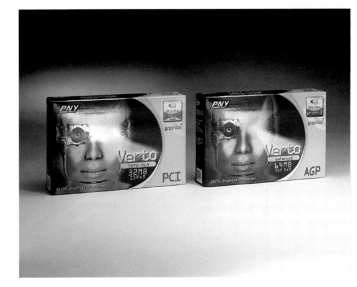

Client
Imagine Foods
Design Firm
Gauger & Silva
Designer
Jamie Duberstein

Client
Harris Teeter
Design Firm
C&M Marketing
Art Director
David Gurman
Designers
Sue Sottile, Jane Atwell

Client
Harris Teeter
Design Firm
C&M Marketing
Art Director
David Gurman
Designer
Joanne Sena Hines
Illustrator
Judy Unger

Client
Johnson & Johnson Consumer Products Co.
Design Firm
LMS Design, Inc.
Designers
Pam Shear, Richard Shear

Client
Playtex Products, Inc.
Design Firm
Tom Fowler, Inc.
Designers
Elizabeth P. Ball, Pamela Kehlenbach

Client
Weight Watchers International
Design Firm
Zunda Design Group
Designer
Charles Zunda

Client
DCI
Design Firm
DCI
Designers
Andy Thorington, Renee Thorington
Illustrator
Steve Lavigne

Client
Dole Food
Design Firm
DuPuis
Designers
Steven DuPuis, Bill Corridori,
John Silva, Jack Halpern,
Al Nanakonpanom

Client
Gillette
Design Firm
Phillips Design Group
Designer
Susan Logcher

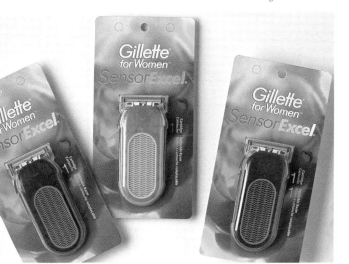

Client
Hasbro
Design Firm
Phillips Design Group
Designers
Alison Goudreault, Beth Parker

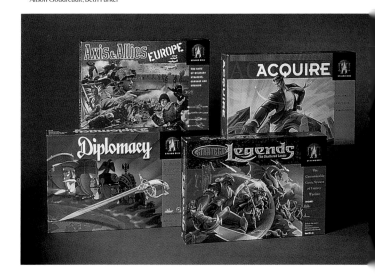

Client
   Unilever
Design Firm
   R.BIRD
Designers
   Joseph Favata, Michele Li

Client
   Barbara's Bakery
Design Firm
   Gauger & Silva
Designer
   Lori Murphy

Client
   C. Shoemaker
Design Firm
   Adam, Filippo & Associates
Designers
   Martin Perez, Robert Adam

Client
   Huffy Bicycle Company
Design Firm
   VMA
Designers
   Greg Fehrenbach,
   Al Hidalgo,
   Joel Warneke

Client
  Newman's Own, Inc.
Design Firm
  Zunda Design Group
Designer
  Todd Nickel, Charles Zunda

Client
  Puget Sound Energy
Design Firm
  Greg Welsh Design
Designer
  Greg Welsh

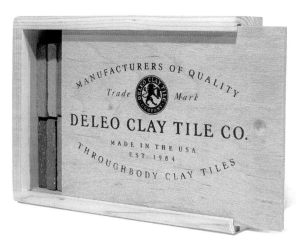

Client
  Deleo Clay Tile Company
Design Firm
  Mires
Creative Director
  José Serrano
Designer
  Gale Spitzley

Client
  Hasbro
Design Firm
  Mires Design
Creative Director
  John Ball
Designer
  David Adey
Illustrator
  Jeff Samaripa

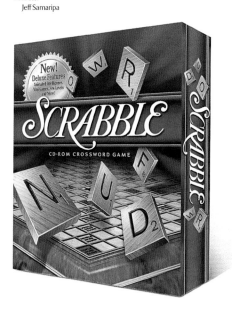

LETTERHEADS

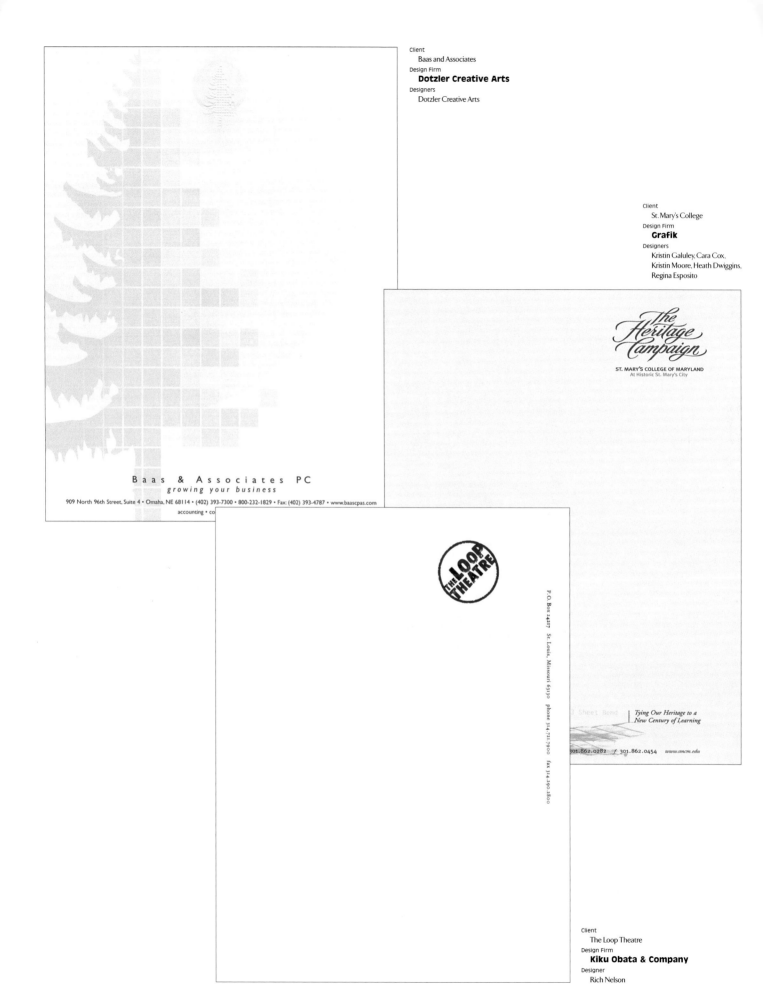

Client
Baas and Associates
Design Firm
Dotzler Creative Arts
Designers
Dotzler Creative Arts

Client
St. Mary's College
Design Firm
Grafik
Designers
Kristin Galuley, Cara Cox,
Kristin Moore, Heath Dwiggins,
Regina Esposito

Baas & Associates PC
growing your business
909 North 96th Street, Suite 4 • Omaha, NE 68114 • (402) 393-7300 • 800-232-1829 • Fax: (402) 393-4787 • www.baascpas.com
accounting • co

ST. MARY'S COLLEGE OF MARYLAND
At Historic St. Mary's City

*Tying Our Heritage to a
New Century of Learning*

P.O. Box 24217 St. Louis, Missouri 63130   phone 314.721.7900   fax 314.290.2800

301.862.0282   f 301.862.0454   www.smcm.edu

Client
The Loop Theatre
Design Firm
Kiku Obata & Company
Designer
Rich Nelson

Client
KSI Corporation
Design Firm
**Emphasis Seven
Communications, Inc.**
Designer
Craig Niedermaier

303 E Army Trail Rd. Suite 110
Bloomingdale IL 60108
ksi-corp.com
t: 630.980.1111
f: 630.980.7049

KSI
corporation

reaching beyond borders

education on safari

21 ames terroce
camden maine
04843 usa
1.207.236.9878
info@reachingbeyondborders.com

www.reachingbeyondborders.com

Client
Reaching Beyond Borders
Design Firm
DW Group
Creative Director
Roberta Greany
Designers
Erin Flett, Rosanne Romiglio

COMPASS PRIVATE BANKING
Stay close to go far

ompass Place

Bedford

chusetts 0274

084-6561

084-6575

ampassbank.com

Client
Compass Bank
Design Firm
Doerr Associates
Designer
Lauren Jeuick

Client
Briley & Stables Creative
Design Firm
Briley & Stables Creative
Designers
Dan Stables, Terry Briley

BRILEY & STABLES CREATIVE

2011 N. COLLINS • SUITE 709 • RICHARDSSON, TEXAS 75080 • 972-470-9595 P • 972-437-3664 F

ANCHOR
Club

THE ANCHOR CLUB AT GRAND HARBOR   325 C.R. 380, BOX 1003, COUNCE, TN 38326
ph: 731.689.2500 www.theanchorclub.com

Client
DW Group
Design Firm
DW Group
Creative Director
Roberta Greany
Art Directors
Roberta Greany, Robert Brochu
Designer
Erin Flett

Client
Anchor Group
Design Firm
Gouthier Design, Inc.
Designers
Jonathan J. Gouthier, Marina Fagerstrom

Client
California College of Arts and Crafts
Design Firm
Aufuldish & Warinner
Designer
Bob Aufuldish

CCAC
1111 **Eighth** STREET
San Francisco, CA 94107
415.703.9500
www.ccac-art.edu

California College of **Arts** and **Crafts**
San Francisco/Oakland
ART **Architecture Design**

T 703 819 1799
F 703 467 0538

Computer Security Consultants
1497 Autumn Ridge Circle
Reston, Virginia 20194
info@digitaldefenders.com

DIGITAL DEFENDERS

www.digitaldefenders.com

Client
The Home Connection
Design Firm
Sayles Graphic Design
Designer
John Sayles

Client
Digital Defenders
Design Firm
Grasp Creative
Designer
Doug Fuller, Aaron Taylor

111

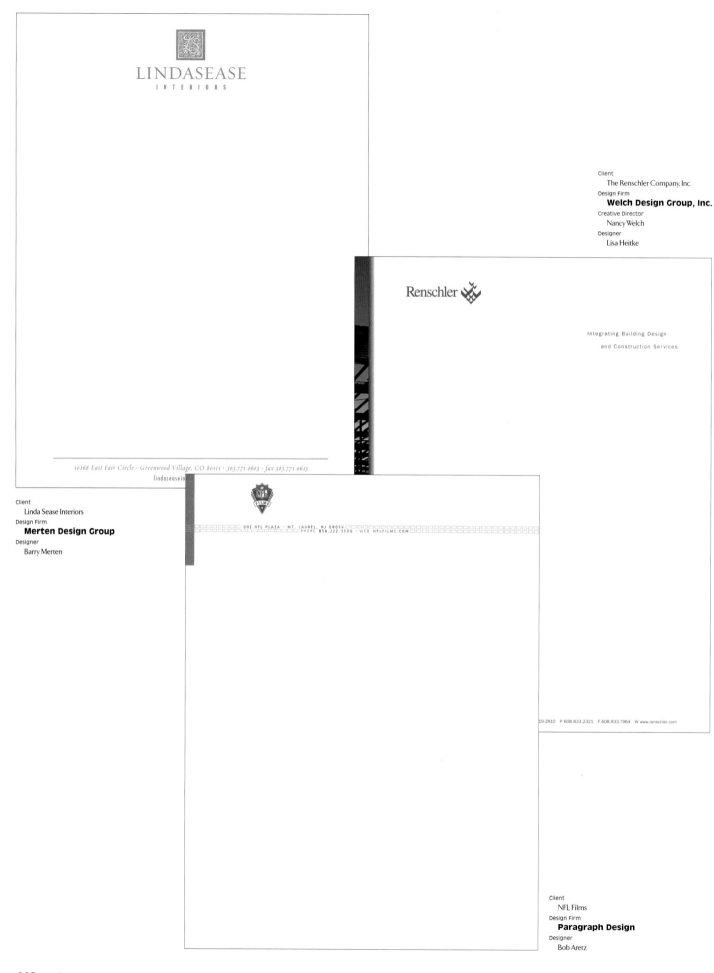

LINDASEASE
INTERIORS

10168 East Fair Circle · Greenwood Village, CO 80111 · 303.771.0603 · fax 303.771.0613
lindaseasein

Renschler ❦

Integrating Building Design
and Construction Services

ONE NFL PLAZA · MT. LAUREL, NJ 08054
PHONE 856.222.3500 · WEB NFLFILMS.COM

19-2810   P 608.833.2321   F 608.833.7964   W www.renschler.com

Client
The Renschler Company, Inc.
Design Firm
Welch Design Group, Inc.
Creative Director
Nancy Welch
Designer
Lisa Heitke

Client
Linda Sease Interiors
Design Firm
Merten Design Group
Designer
Barry Merten

Client
NFL Films
Design Firm
Paragraph Design
Designer
Bob Aretz

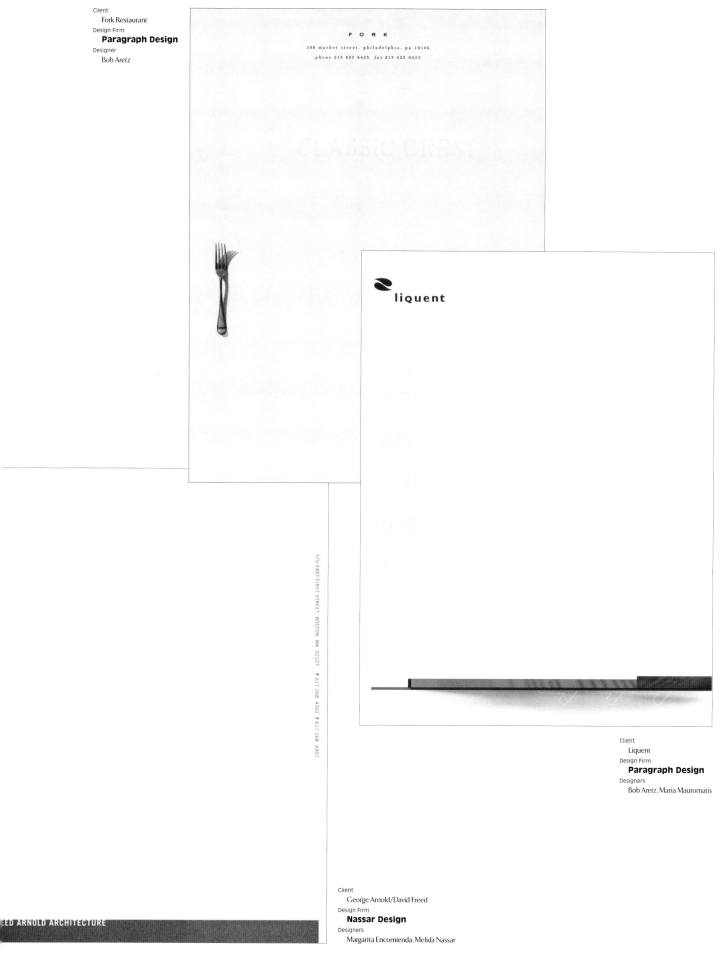

Client
Fork Restaurant
Design Firm
Paragraph Design
Designer
Bob Aretz

F O R K

306 market street, philadelphia, pa 19106

phone 215 625 9425 *fax* 215 625 9435

liquent

570 EAST FIRST STREET BOSTON MA 02127 P 617 268 4302 F 617 268 4307

ED ARNOLD ARCHITECTURE

Client
Liquent
Design Firm
Paragraph Design
Designers
Bob Aretz, Maria Mauromatis

Client
George Arnold/David Freed
Design Firm
Nassar Design
Designers
Margarita Encomienda, Melida Nassar

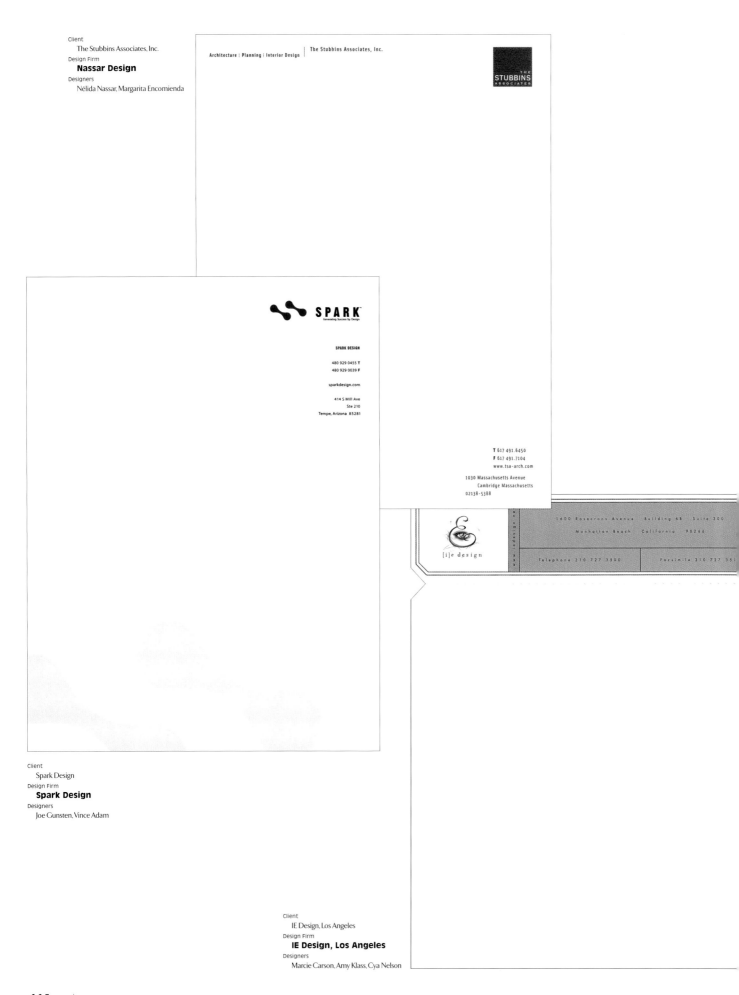

Client
The Stubbins Associates, Inc.
Design Firm
Nassar Design
Designers
Nélida Nassar, Margarita Encomienda

Architecture | Planning | Interior Design | The Stubbins Associates, Inc.

THE
STUBBINS
ASSOCIATES

SPARK
Generating Success by Design

SPARK DESIGN

480 929 0455 **T**
480 929 0039 **F**

sparkdesign.com

414 S Mill Ave
Ste 210
Tempe, Arizona 85281

T 617 491.6450
F 617 491.7104
www.tsa-arch.com

1030 Massachusetts Avenue
Cambridge Massachusetts
02138-5388

[i]e design

1600 Rosecrans Avenue   Building 6B   Suite 200
Manhattan Beach   California   90266

Telephone 310.727.3500   Facsimile 310.727.351

Client
Spark Design
Design Firm
Spark Design
Designers
Joe Gunsten, Vince Adam

Client
IE Design, Los Angeles
Design Firm
IE Design, Los Angeles
Designers
Marcie Carson, Amy Klass, Cya Nelson

Client
Lemley Design Company
Design Firm
Lemley Design Company
Designers
David Lemley, Tawnya Lemley

LEMLEYИ⅁I2ƎD

LEMLEY DESIGN COMPANY
ADDRESS 8 BOSTON STREET, #17, SEATTLE, WA 98109, USA
TELEPHONE 206 385 6900 / FACSIMILE 206 285 6900 / INTERNET www.lemleydesign.com

Client
Arz Travel, Inc.
Design Firm
Nassar Design
Designers
Nélida Nassar, Margaritá Encomienda

arz. **Travel Inc.**   THE DESIGN OF WORLD TRAVEL

**Gables
International
Plaza**

2655
LeJeune Road
Suite 202

Coral Gables
Florida 33134

Telephone
1800 279 . 8728
305 461 . 0101
Telefax
305 461 . 5773
email
farid@arztravel.com

SCHOOL COMMUNITIES THAT WORK

*A National Task
Force on the Future
of Urban Districts*

475 Fifth Avenue
14th Floor
New York, NY 10017
T 212.213.3709
F 212.213.9829

Brown University
Box 1985
Providence, RI 02912
T 401.863.1897
F 401.863.1290

www.aisr.brown.edu

An Initiative of The Annenberg Institute for School Reform

Client
School Communities That Work
Design Firm
Re: Creative
Designers
Tim Eng, Johnny Chau

Client
  Lotus Shipping Agencies
Design Firm
  Nassar Design
Designers
  Nélida Nassar, Margaritá Encomienda

LOTÜS DENİZCİLİK TAŞIMACILIK TİC. LTD. ŞTİ

NASSAR DESIGN

11 Park Street Suite 1 Brookline MA 02446
Telephone 617.264.2862 Telefax 617.264.2861 email nnassar@shore.net

Caddesi   Zincirlikuyu 80300   Telefon (90.212) 216.2002
                 İstanbul   Telefax (90.212) 212.9838
                 Turkey   e-mail lotus.ist@seahorsenet.com

Client
  Nassar Design
Design Firm
  Nassar Design
Designers
  Nélida Nassar, Margaritá Encomienda

NASSAR DESIGN

Client
Sightward
Design Firm
Graphiti Assoc. Inc.
Designer
Kevin Berger

S I G H T W A R D™
power from prediction

results

10800 NE 8th, Suite 200, Bellevue, Washington 98004 (tel) 425.688.9921

THE SAFEST DISTANCE BETWEEN TWO POINTS™

AirSea™
PACKING

AirSea Packing Group Inc.   www.airseapacking.com
8515 South La Cienega Blvd.   t 310.649.0892
Inglewood, CA 90301, USA   f 310.649.0894

Client
AirSea Packing Group, Ltd.
Design Firm
Schnider & Yoshina Ltd.
Designer
Lesley Kunikis

PERFORMANCE PLACE

SECOND & MAIN DAYTON, OHIO 45402 937.224.4395

Client
Second & Main
Design Firm
Graphica
Designers
Susan Doren Kemper,
Cindy Schnell, Leslie Trimbach

Client
Atelier des Architectes Associes
Design Firm
Nassar Design
Designers
Margaritá Encomienda, Nélida Nassar

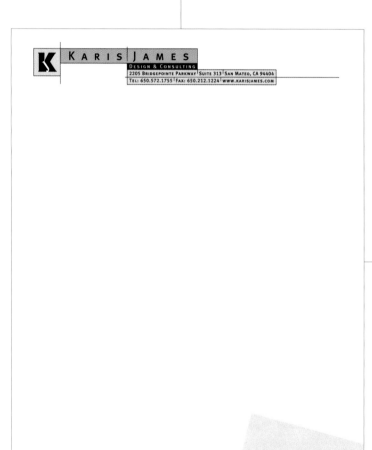

Client
Karis/James
Design Firm
Bruce Yelaska Design
Designer
Bruce Yelaska

Client
Rene Stern/Windermere Real Estate
Design Firm
Lemley Design Company
Designers
David Lemley, Yuri Shvets

Client
Beaulieu Vineyard Wine Society
Design Firm
Halleck
Designer
Wayne Wright

Beaulieu Vineyard.
WINE *Society*

BEAULIEU VINEYARD

POST OFFICE BOX 534

RUTHERFORD, CA 94573

TEL 800 373 5896

FAX 707 967 0558

WWW.BVWINE.COM

Client
Coastal Leasing, Inc.
Design Firm
Nassar Design
Designer
Nélida Nassar

Coastal Leasing, Inc.

179 Sidney Street
Cambridge, Massachusetts 02139

Telephone 617 497.1122
Telefax 617 497.1188

QUEST PARTNERS LLC

126 East 56th Street
19th Floor
New York NY 10022

Telephone 212 838.7222
Telefax 212 838.4440
www.questpartnersllc.com

Client
Quest Partners LLC
Design Firm
Nassar Design
Designers
Nélida Nassar, Margaritá Encomienda

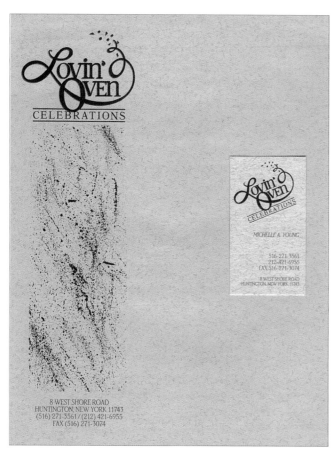

Client
  Lovin Oven Catering
Design Firm
  Callery & Company
Designer
  Kelley Callery

deka design

1133 broadway
suite 1011
new york ny 10010

voice 646.230.6086
fax 646.230.6085
www dekadesign.com

Client
  Deka Design Inc.
Design Firm
  Deka Design
Designer
  Dmitry Krasny

181 South Murphy Avenue ▪ Sunnyvale CA 94086

Telephone 408 736 3731 ▪ Facsimile 408 736 1217

Client
  Tao Tao Chinese Cuisine
Design Firm
  Julia Tam Design
Designer
  Julia Chong Tam

9 2 0 0   RT.   1 0 8,   STE.   2 0 9   ■   COL
W W W .

750 St. Paul Street Rochester, New York 14605 585-546-8868 1-800-799-8868 Fax: 585-546-4918 Web: www.rapidac.com

525 Mayacama Club Drive   Santa Rosa, California 95403   Tel 707.543.8040   Fax 707.543.8094   www.mayacama.com

The Times Building, Third Floor
336 Fourth Avenue
Pittsburgh, Pennsylvania 15222

412.281.1060
Fax 412.281.0177

design solutions that communicate

استيكو

اسـتـيـكــو لإدارة الـمـمـتـلـكـات (ذ.م.م)
Asteco Property Management (L.L.C.)
www.astecoproperty.com
Paid Up Capital AED 300, 000

P.O. Box 1714, **Dubai**, UAE
Tel.: 04-2693155 Fax: 04-2692548
asteco@astecoproperty.com

P.O. Box 45640, **Abu Dhabi**, UAE
Tel.: 02-6262660 Fax: 02-6261923
abudhabi@astecoproperty.com

ZGraphics, Ltd. 322 North River Street, East Dundee, Illinois 60118
847.836.6022 fax 847.836.6122 info@zgraphics.com www.zgraphics.com

Client
Barb's Studio 104
Design Firm
ZGraphics, Ltd.
Art Director
LouAnn Zeller
Designer
Kris Martinez Farrell

104 North River Street │ East Dundee, IL 60118 │ tel 847/428-4433 │ nails 428-4408

Client
Spectrum Engineering, Inc.
Design Firm
Bullet Communications, Inc.
Designer
Timothy Scott Kump

633 Skokie Boulevard
Suite 350
Northbrook, Illinois 60062

Tel: 847.753.9640
Fax: 847.753.9644
E-Mail: Mail@SpectrumE.com

Web: www.SpectrumE.com

Spectrum
ENGINEERING, INC.
ELECTRICAL CONSULTANTS

TRANSOCEAN
CAPITAL, INC.

Strathmore
PURE COTTON

One Boston Place • 5th Floor • Boston, MA 02108 • ph.617.367.7900 • fx.617.619.3526

Client
Transocean Capital
Design Firm
Cottrill Design
Designer
Allison Cottrill

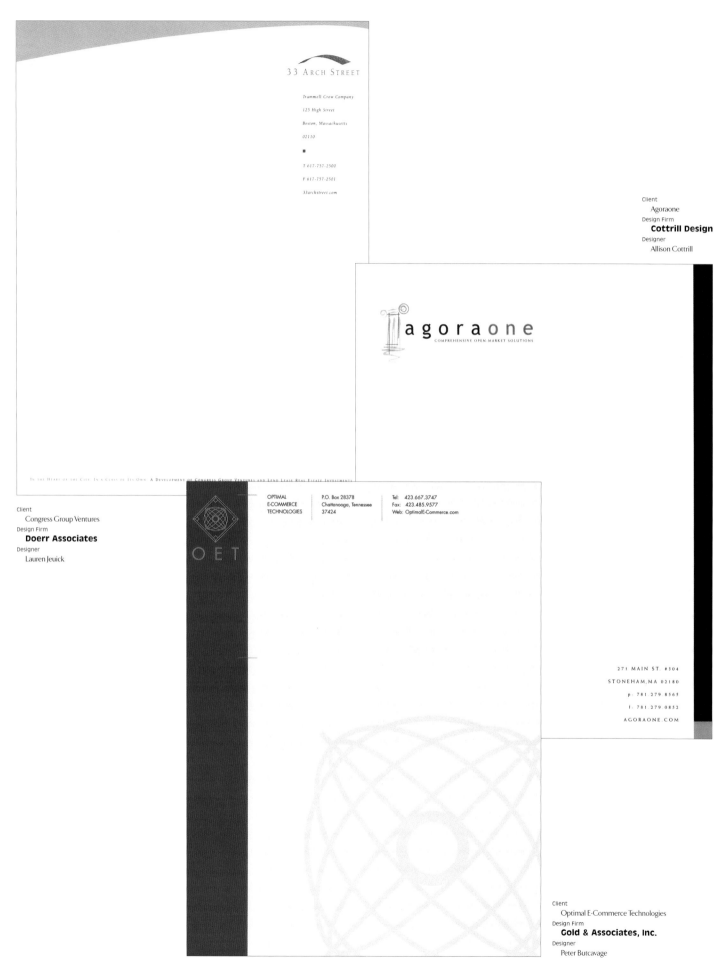

33 ARCH STREET

Trammell Crow Company
125 High Street
Boston, Massachusetts
02110

■

T 617-757-2500
F 617-757-2501
33archstreet.com

IN THE HEART OF THE CITY. IN A CLASS OF ITS OWN. A DEVELOPMENT OF CONGRESS GROUP VENTURES AND LEND LEASE REAL ESTATE INVESTMENTS

Client
Agoraone
Design Firm
Cottrill Design
Designer
Allison Cottrill

agoraone
COMPREHENSIVE OPEN-MARKET SOLUTIONS

Client
Congress Group Ventures
Design Firm
Doerr Associates
Designer
Lauren Jeuick

OPTIMAL
E-COMMERCE
TECHNOLOGIES

P.O. Box 28378
Chattanooga, Tennessee
37424

Tel: 423.667.3747
Fax: 423.485.9577
Web: OptimalE-Commerce.com

OET

271 MAIN ST. #304
STONEHAM, MA 02180
p: 781.279 8565
f: 781.279 0852
AGORAONE.COM

Client
Optimal E-Commerce Technologies
Design Firm
Gold & Associates, Inc.
Designer
Peter Butcavage

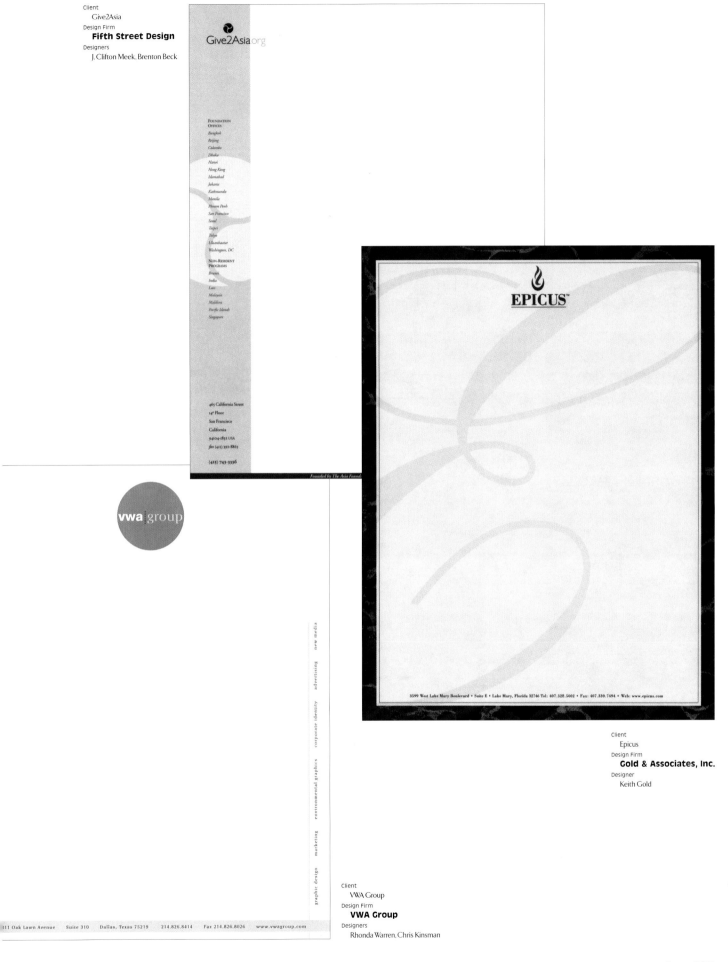

Client
Give2Asia

Design Firm
Fifth Street Design

Designers
J. Clifton Meek, Brenton Beck

Give2Asia.org

FOUNDATION
OFFICES
Bangkok
Beijing
Colombo
Dhaka
Hanoi
Hong Kong
Islamabad
Jakarta
Kathmandu
Manila
Phnom Penh
San Francisco
Seoul
Taipei
Tokyo
Ulaanbaatar
Washington, DC

NON-RESIDENT
PROGRAMS
Brunei
India
Laos
Malaysia
Maldives
Pacific Islands
Singapore

465 California Street
14th Floor
San Francisco
California
94104-1832 USA
fax (415) 392-8863

(415) 743-3336

Founded by The Asia Found...

EPICUS™

3599 West Lake Mary Boulevard • Suite E • Lake Mary, Florida 32746 Tel: 407.328.5002 • Fax: 407.330.7494 • Web: www.epicus.com

Client
Epicus

Design Firm
Gold & Associates, Inc.

Designer
Keith Gold

vwa group

graphic design   marketing   environmental graphics   corporate identity   advertising   new media

311 Oak Lawn Avenue   Suite 310   Dallas, Texas 75219   214.826.8414   Fax 214.826.8026   www.vwagroup.com

Client
VWA Group

Design Firm
VWA Group

Designers
Rhonda Warren, Chris Kinsman

125

Client
Fly in My Soup Entertainment
Design Firm
Garrison Design
Designer
Richard Garrison
Illustrator
Greg Preslicka

DIVERSITY TRAINING

EDUCATIONAL WORKSHOPS

CORPORATE ENTERTAINMENT

PRIVATE ENTERTAINMENT

STAGE PRODUCTIONS

601 WAYZATA BOULEVARD • MINNEAPOLIS MN 55426-1637

87 • 1-866-FLY-SOUP (359-7687) • FAX 952 . 345 . 7689 • www.flyinmysoupent.com

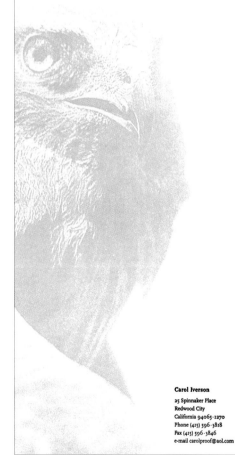

HAWKEYE PROOFREADING

Professional proofreading & copyediting

Carol Iverson

25 Spinnaker Place
Redwood City
California 94065·1270
Phone (415) 596·3818
Fax (415) 596·3846
e-mail carolproof@aol.com

Client
Hawkeye Proofreading
Design Firm
tompertdesign
Designers
Claudia Huber Tompert,
Michael Tompert

Client
TwinEngines
Design Firm
Jones Design Group
Designer
Vicky Jones

TwinEngines™

Microsoft Certified
Solution Provider

pplication Development

www.twinengines.com

Client
Design North
Design Firm
Design North
Design Director
Richard Jacobs
Creative Director
Gwen Granzow

Design North

BRANDING FOR THE
RETAIL ENVIRONMENT

Design North, Inc.
www.designnorth.com

Midwest
8007 Douglas Avenue
Racine, Wisconsin 53402

Phone 262.639.2080
Toll Free 800.247.8494
Fax 262.639.5230

West
One Tabor Center
1200 17th Street
Suite 1000
Denver, Colorado 80202

Phone 303.893.2280
Fax 303.893.2281

Alacritus™
SOFTWARE

Client
Alacritus
Design Firm
Dickson Design
Designer
Deborah Shea

Alacritus Software
1650 Holmes Street
Livermore, CA 94550
925.960.0695
925.960.0692 FAX
www.alacritus.com

T 650.325.9600
F 650.325.9608

SUITE 305
505 HAMILTON AVENUE
PALO ALTO, CA 94301

www.comven.com

COMVENTURES

Client
ComVentures
Design Firm
Gee + Chung Design
Designers
Earl Gee, Fani Chung

Client
Abacuss Apparel Group
Design Firm
X Design Company
Designers
Alex Valderrama, Jen Dahlen

15580 East Hinsdale Circle • Englewood • Colorado 80112 • 877.680.9484 • FAX 877.680.9485

Standard Process
of Northern California, Inc.

6201 Doyle Street, Suite A, Emeryville, California 94608 **email** info@spnatural.com **fax** (510) 597-9106 **voice** (510) 597-9100

Client
Standard Process of Northern California
Design Firm
Fifth Street Design
Designers
Brenton Beck, J. Clifton Meek

Client
Milestone Construction Management
Design Firm
X Design Company
Designers
Alex Valderrama, Jan Dahlen

MILESTONE
CONSTRUCTION MANAGEMENT

WWW.MILESTONECM.COM   12649 EAST CAL

R I M U   G R O V E   W I N E R Y   L T D

B e n n i e F a c t o r   P r o d u c t s

Brearc Road East ◆ RD1 Upper Moutere ◆ Nelson, New Zealand ◆ email rimugrove@xtra.co.nz ◆ voice/fax +64-3-540 2345

Client
Rimu Grove Winery Ltd.
Design Firm
Fifth Street Design
Designers
J. Clifton Meek,
Lisa Camp de Avalos

Client
BennieFactor Products
Design Firm
Route 8, A Design Firm
Art Director
Janet Rauscher
Designer
Russ Jackson

Client
American Forest Defense Fund
Design Firm
McGaughy Design
Designer
Malcolm McGaughy

AMERICAN FOREST DEFENSE FUND

THE PERRY

AT CABRINI CENTER

The Perry is sponsored by the Missionary Sisters of the Sacred Heart of Jesus

901 Boren Avenue, Suite 1600, Seattle, Washington 98104 Phone:206.652.4400 Fax:206.652.1424

Client
The Perry at Cabrini Center
Design Firm
Coakley Heagerty
Designers
Robert Meyerson, Randy Jones

Client
Alice Cooper Celebrity AM
Design Firm
Rule 29
Designers
Justin Ahrens, Jim Boborci

Client
Philip Anthony Salon
Design Firm
BBK Studio
Designers
Alison Popp, Kevin Budelmann

PHILIP ANTHONY

APIDS MI 49546   616 464 1311

Client
Tammy Nystuen
Design Firm
Peggy Lauritsen Design Group
Designer
Laura Dokken

n.

Nystuen
communications

phone **763.780.2234**   fax **763.780.2238**

North County
HUMANE
SOCIETY
& SPCA

together we will be kind to animals
North County Humane Society & SPCA
2905 San Luis Rey Road • Oceanside, California 92054
www.nchumane.org   tel 760.757.4357 • fax 760.757.3547

Client
North County Humane Society
Design Firm
Winter Advertising Agency
Designer
Mary Winter

Client
Artimas
Design Firm
**Rosetta Advertising
and Public Relations**
Designer
Lori Lucas

Client
Fiercely Independent Films
Design Firm
Creative Dynamics, Inc.
Designers
Mackenzie Walsh, Victor Rodriguez

Client
Wiseman Images
Design Firm
Communication Via Design
Designers
Christine Corso,
Maggie Sanftleben

Client
Chatham Seafarer
Design Firm
Communication Via Design
Designers
Vicki Adjami, Nisha Shrestha

Å
2079 Main Street Chatham Massachusetts 02633-1020
www.chathamseafarer.com ⇐ ——⊹—— ⇒ e-mail seafarer@cape.com
tel 800 786-2772 508 432-1739 fax 508 432-8969
Y

chatham seafarer

ENGINEERED FOR BUSINESS DESIGNED FOR YOU

the **krone** group LLC
commercial real estate services

225 South Sixth Street, Suite 3434 • Minneapolis, Minnesota 55402 • Phone: 612.672.3011 Fax: 612.672.3015 e-mail: hines@225southsixth.com

Client
Hines
Design Firm
Shea
Designers
Viera Hartmannova,
James Rahn

2101 richmond road
beachwood oh 44122

216 464-5900
216 464-3128 fax

www.thekronegroup.com

member of International Council of Shopping Centers

Client
The Krone Group
Design Firm
Crawford Design
Designer
Alison Crawford

Client
Seattle Convention &
Visitors Bureau
Design Firm
**Hornall Anderson
Design Works**
Designers
Lisa Cerveny, Jack Anderson,
Bruce Branson-Meyer,
Mark Popich

Intelsat
inspiring connections

and Visitors Bureau

tle.org

oo, Seattle, WA 98101

206 461 5855

WORDS BY DESIGN

3400 International Drive NW, Washington DC 20008-3006 USA www.intelsat.com T +1 202-944-6800 F +1 202-944-7898

Client
Intelsat
Design Firm
Addison
Designers
Tina Antonopoulos,
David Kohler

Client
Words By Design
Design Firm
Hausman Design, Inc.
Designer
Joan L. Hausman

102 WAVERLEY STREET, SUITE 308
PALO ALTO, CALIFORNIA 94301
TEL 650 322 0340 FAX 650 322 0341
www.wordsbydesign.com

Client
    University Children's Foundation
Design Firm
    Liz J. Design, Inc.
Designer
    Bryan Barnes

May 17-18, 2002
Minneapolis Convention Center

WineFest No. 7
The Seventh Annual
Benefit of the University
Children's Foundation

WineFest
c/o UCF
MMC 727
420 Delaware Street SE
Minneapolis, MN 55455
PH 612.625.1471
FX 612.626.1144

Client
    Rosetta Advertising and
    Public Relations
Design Firm
    **Rosetta Advertising and
    Public Relations**
Designer
    Bill White

Rosetta
Advertising & Public Relations, LLC

Indianapolis
Louisville
Terre Haute
www.rosetta-adpr.com

328 South Fifth Street • P.O. Box 2326 • T

P.O. BOX 55995, SHERMAN OAKS, CA 91413

Client
    The Elizabeth Taylor AIDS Foundation
Design Firm
    Biondo Group
Designer
    Stephen Longo

Client
    Autumn Associates, Inc.
Design Firm
dsgn associates
Design Director
    C. Cal Young, AIA
Designer
    Nancy P. Weeks

○○○
a u t u m n
associates, inc.

ARCSOURCE
TECHNOLOGY · CONSULTING

2648 Stuart Street | Berkeley, CA 94705 | 510.843.2010
info@arcsource.net | www.arcsource.net

winchester, ohio 43110 . 614 560 3714
.com

Client
    Arc Source Technology Consulting
Design Firm
Jiva Creative
Designer
    Eric Lee

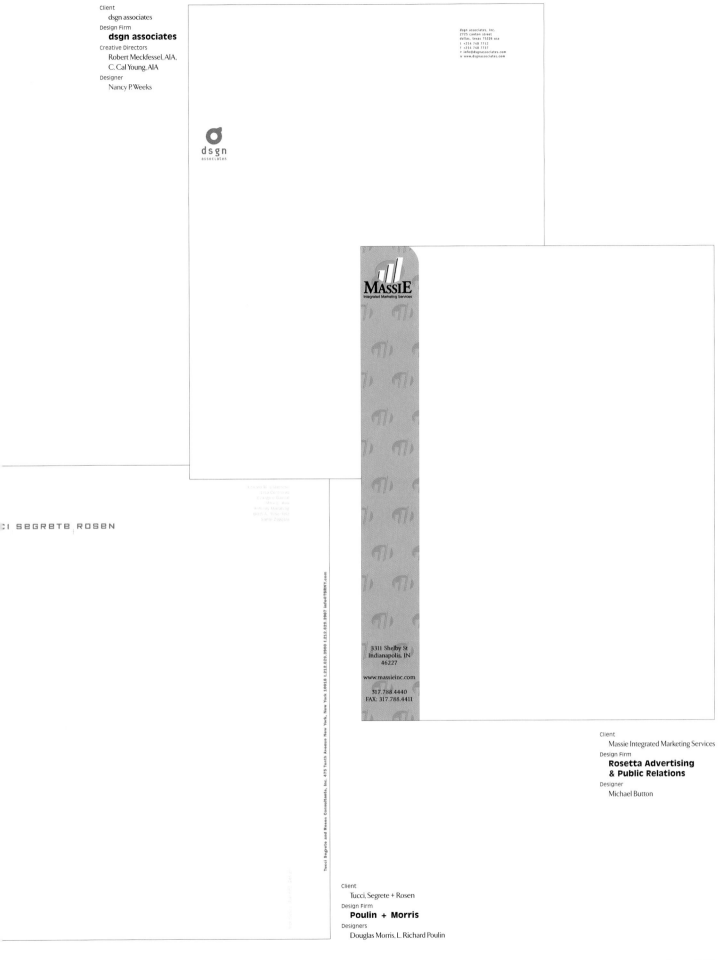

Client
dsgn associates
Design Firm
dsgn associates
Creative Directors
Robert Meckfessel, AIA,
C. Cal Young, AIA
Designer
Nancy P. Weeks

dsgn associates, inc.
2725 canton street
dallas, texas 75226 usa
t +214 748 7712
f +214 748 7737
e info@dsgnassociates.com
w www.dsgnassociates.com

dsgn
associates

CI SEGRETE ROSEN

Tucci Segrete and Rosen Consultants, Inc. 475 Tenth Avenue New York, New York 10018 t.212.629.3900 f.212.629.3907 info@TSRNY.com

MASSIE
Integrated Marketing Services

3311 Shelby St
Indianapolis, IN
46227

www.massieinc.com

317.788.4440
FAX: 317.788.4411

Client
Massie Integrated Marketing Services
Design Firm
**Rosetta Advertising
& Public Relations**
Designer
Michael Button

Client
Tucci, Segrete + Rosen
Design Firm
Poulin + Morris
Designers
Douglas Morris, L. Richard Poulin

Client
Uptown Community Action Group
Design Firm
Adam, Filippo & Associates
Designers
Adam, Filippo & Associates

1643 Fifth Avenue
Pittsburgh, PA 15219
Phone: 412.201.1232
Fax: 412.201.1233
Email: Uptownaction@aol.com

PROMISTAR

FINANCIAL

gh awareness and involvement

COMMUNITY
BANKING

GLOBAL
VISION

fORD
CONSULTING
GROUP

minneapolis
212 THIRD AVENUE NORTH
SUITE 385
MINNEAPOLIS, MN 55401-1445
612-333-1111 phone
612-333-1112 fax

los angeles
880 APOLLO STREET
SUITE 206
EL SEGUNDO, CA 90245-4783
310-414-3000 phone
310-414-4500 fax

FORDCONSULTINGGROUP.COM

Promistar Plaza 551 Main Street Johnstown Pennsylvania 15901 tel 814 532 3801 fax 814 536 2278 www.promistar.com

Client
Promistar Financial
Design Firm
Adam, Filippo & Associates
Designers
Martin Perez, Robert Adam

Client
Ford Consulting Group
Design Firm
Tilka Design
Designer
Sarah Steil

DELEO CLAY TILE COMPANY
MANUFACTURERS OF THROUGHBODY TILES

600 Chaney Street · Lake Elsinore · California · 92530
Telephone 909 674 1578 · 800 654 1119 · Fax 909 245 2427
www.deleoclaytile.com

Senses
S P A

PO box F-42500   T: +242 350 5281
Royal Palm Way   F: +242 350 5280
Lucaya   E: spa@ourlucaya.com
Grand Bahama Island   www.ourlucaya.com

p.b.solutions
A View From Experience

>> **PREFERRED BUSINESS SOLUTIONS, LLC**   John J. Hennessy
   SOLVING   *Principal*
   BUSINESS
   PROBLEMS

>> 224 MOUNTWELL AVENUE | HADDONFIELD, NJ 08033 | PHONE: 856.795.0034   PFDBIZ@AOL.COM

harter & associates
enrolled agents, the tax specialists

120 West Oregon Avenue
Phoenix, Arizona 85013
tel 602 266 7167
fax 602 266 7168

Client
Mizrahi Design Associates, Inc.
Design Firm
Mizrahi Design Associates, Inc.
Creative Director
Laurie Mizrahi
Designer
Brad Ireland

650 SMITHFIELD ST. | SUITE 1525 | PITTSBURGH, PA 15222
P 412 281 5025 | 412 281 5056 www.mizrahidesign.com

MIZRAHI DESIGN ASSOCIATES, INC.

Client
Harter & Associates
Design Firm
Spark Design
Designer
Rik Boberg

1953 GALLOWS ROAD, 5TH FLOOR, VIENNA, VA, 22182
T 703 734 9200 · 800 397 7561 · F 703 734 6565

BIONETRIX SYSTEMS CORPORATION

WWW.BIONETRIX.COM

Bio·Netrix

NEWS RELEASE

communication planning
and **design**

Client
BioNetrix
Design Firm
Grafik
Designers
Kristin Moore,
Franciska Guenther

Client
C. Shoemaker
Design Firm
Adam, Filippo & Associates
Designers
Martin Perey, Robert Adam

INVESTMENT CONSULTING

YANNI
PARTNERS

DELIVERING THE PROMISE
■ ■ ■
310 Grant Street, Pittsburgh, PA 15219-2302 412.232.1000 Fax 412.232.1022 www.yannipartners.com

Client
The Silicon Oasis.com
Design Firm
Brand, Ltd.
Designer
Scott Wizell

Client
Yanni Partners
Design Firm
Adam, Filippo & Associates
Designers
Martin Perez, Robert Adam

Client
  Precision Translating Services
Design Firm
  Original Impressions
Designer
  Mike Blount

150 WEST FLAGLER ST. • MUSEUM TOWER
PENTHOUSE II • MIAMI, FLORIDA 33130
TEL 305 373•7874 **FAX** 381•7874
TOLL FREE: 1 (888) 304•7874
E-MAIL: generalmail@pretran.com

1280 South Clayton Street / Denver Colorado 80210 / T 303-691-9000 / F 303-691-9229 / www.insite-design-group.com

Client
  In.Site Design
Design Firm
  Noble Erickson Inc
Designers
  Robin H. Ridley, Jackie Noble

"At Christmas, we
collected books for
needy kids."

Christopher • Cub Scout Pack 42
McLean County

614 N.E. Madison Avenue

Peoria, Illinois 61603-3833

phone: 309/673.6136

1-800/369.5069

fax: 309/673.6184

visit: www.wdboyce.org

Counties served:

Bureau

DeWitt

Ford

Fulton

LaSalle

Livingston

Logan

Marshall

Mason

McLean

Peoria

Putnam

Tazewell

Woodford

*Please support
the United Way.*

Client
  Tracy Techau, Scout Executive, CEO
Designer
  Jennifer Hammontree-Jones

Client
  Pancor Construcion + Development LLC
Design Firm
  Rule 29
Designers
  Justin Ahrens, Jim Boborci

Client
  Blake Real Estate, Inc.
Design Firm
  Sparkman & Associates, Inc.
Designer
  Don Sparkman

PANCOR

B L A K E   R E A L   E S T A T E   I N C

BLAKE

M E M O R A N D U M

Date:

To:

From:

Re:

PANCOR CONSTRUCTION & DEVELOPMENT, LLC.

2250 POINT BOULEVARD | SUITE 125 | ELGIN, IL 60123
T 847 551 9195 / 847 551 9198

1150 Connecticut Avenue, NW •
Telephone: 202.778.04

absorba®

collection bébé de France
100 W 33rd St, Suite 813 - New York, NY 10001
p 212 279 3211 f 212 714 0401 absorba@tawil.com

Client
  Absorba
Design Firm
  Lieber Brewster Design, Inc.
Designers
  Aimee N. Youngs, Elisa Carson

MARK BOLSTER

412.231.3757 T
412.231.0910 F

2200 California Avenue Pittsburgh, Pennsylvania 15212

www.markbolster.com   mbolster@markbolster.com

St. Jane Frances de Chantal
CHURCH

Client
St. Jane Frances de Chantal Church
Design Firm
Graves Fowler Associates
Designer
Victoria Q. Robinson

g f

graves fowler associates

301 530 1550 FAX 301 493 8953 E-MAIL StJane2000@aol.com

Client
Mark Bolster Photography
Design Firm
Mona MacDonald Design
Designer
Mona MacDonald

v 301.816.0097
5515 security lane suite 1109
f 301.816.0947
rockville, md 20852
www.gravesfowler.com

maryland california

Client
Graves Fowler Associates
Design Firm
Graves Fowler Associates
Designers
Dianne C. Burbank,
Victoria Q. Robinson, Elaine Chow

Two Gateway Center 8960 Bay Colony Blvd.
Suite 205 Suite 1804
Pittsburgh, PA 15222 Naples, FL 34108

412.392.3555 tel 941.594.0252 tel
412.355.0483 fax 941.594.1348 fax

TC GRAHAM ASSOCIATES

C M E   P L A N N I N G   M E E T I N G

THE VISITING FACULTY PROGRAM ON
METASTATIC BREAST CANCER

GAMES
OVER

WHERE A NEW SEASON BEGINS

WWW.GAMESOVER.ORG

PO Box 3500, Suite 185   Sisters, OR 97759   Tel (541) 549-8085   Fax (541) 549-8121   Email newseason@gamesover.org

Client
Statler Arms
Design Firm
Karen Skunta & Company
Creative Director
Karen A. Skunta
Designer
Christopher Suster

Statler *Arms*

THE CIVILIZED LIFE

clid Avenue Cleveland, Ohio 44115-1601 216-696-6800 fax: 216-696-6801 www.statlerarms.com

MIAMI BEACH
Marriott.
AT SOUTH BEACH

161 Ocean Drive Miami Beach, Florida 33139 Ph: 305.536.7700 Fx: 305.536.9900

Client
Miami Beach Marriott at South Beach
Design Firm
Gouthier Design, Inc.

Client
Reinnov8
Design Firm
Reinnov8
Designer
Richard A. Hooper

128 Matterhorn Drive
Monroeville, PA 15146
phone: 724.327.8708
info@reinnov8.com
www.reinnov8.com

REINNOV8

Client
Valhalla Restaurant
Design Firm
Dan Liew Design
Designers
Dan Liew, Jet Lim, Linda Kelley

Valhalla

Valhalla
201 Bridgeway
415.332.2777(v)

Southern Tier Library System

580 West Water Street Ext
Painted Post, New York 14870

607.962.3141

607.962.5356

www.stls.org

Client
Southern Tier Library System
Design Firm
Michael Orr & Associates, Inc.
Designers
Michael R. Orr, Scott Dziura

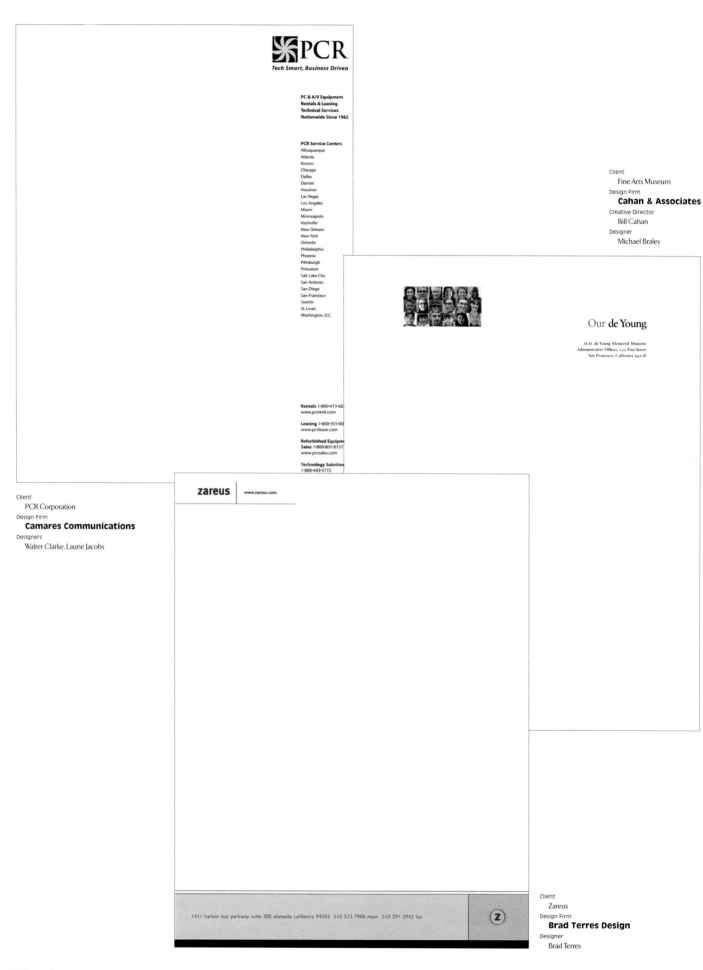

PCR
Tech Smart, Business Driven

PC & A/V Equipment
Rentals & Leasing
Technical Services
Nationwide Since 1982

PCR Service Centers
Albuquerque
Atlanta
Boston
Chicago
Dallas
Detroit
Houston
Las Vegas
Los Angeles
Miami
Minneapolis
Nashville
New Orleans
New York
Orlando
Philadelphia
Phoenix
Pittsburgh
Princeton
Salt Lake City
San Antonio
San Diego
San Francisco
Seattle
St. Louis
Washington, D.C.

Rentals 1·800·473·68
www.pcrrent.com

Leasing 1·800·355·00
www.pcrlease.com

Refurbished Equipm
Sales 1·800·801·8157
www.pcrsales.com

Technology Solution
1·888·443·5772

Our de Young

M.H. de Young Memorial Museum
Administrative Offices, 233 Post Street
San Francisco, California 94108

Client
Fine Arts Museum
Design Firm
Cahan & Associates
Creative Director
Bill Cahan
Designer
Michael Braley

Client
PCR Corporation
Design Firm
Camares Communications
Designers
Walter Clarke, Laurie Jacobs

zareus www.zareus.com

1411 harbor bay parkway suite 200 alameda california 94502 510 523 7900 main 510 291 2942 fax

Client
Zareus
Design Firm
Brad Terres Design
Designer
Brad Terres

WORLD-CLASS CABARET

S I L K
NEW YORK

552 WEST 38TH STREET ▪ NEW YORK, NY 10018

MedEWay
MedEWay.com, Inc.
Two Concourse Pkwy
Suite 810
Atlanta, GA 30303-5588

VENTURA
MARBLE

phone 702 [34] 9445] fax 702 [34] 9447] 981 w. charleston suite 2-352 las vegas, nevada 89117 lic.# 52248/52228

78.320.0076
78.320.0625

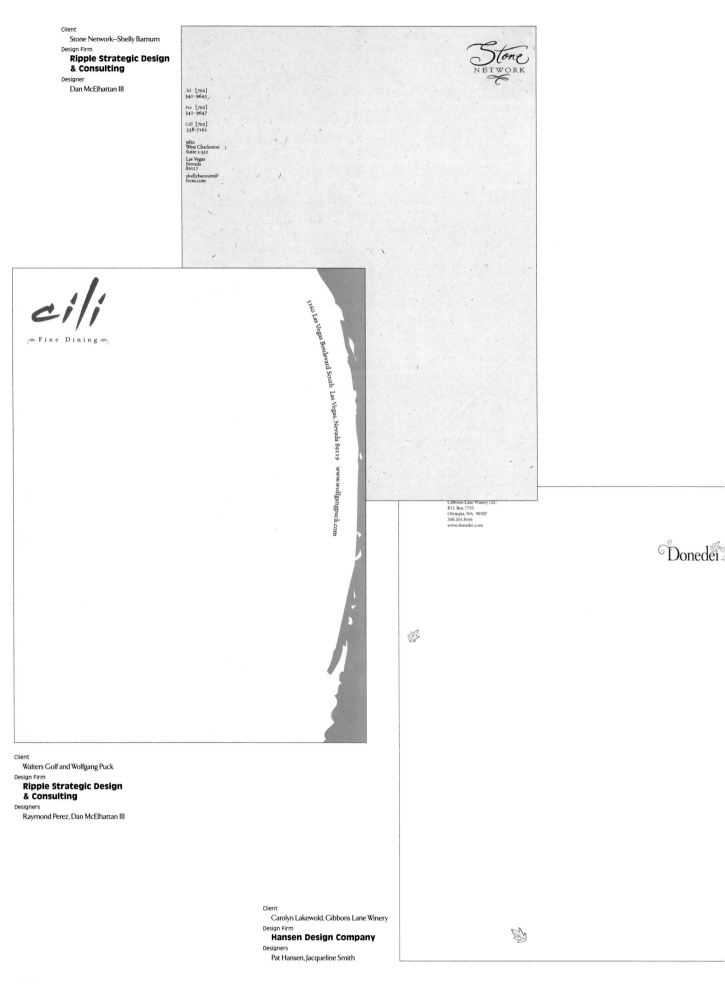

Client
Stone Network–Shelly Barnum
Design Firm
**Ripple Strategic Design
& Consulting**
Designer
Dan McElhattan III

Tel [702]
341-9645

Fax [702]
341-9647

Cell [702]
338-7161

9811
West Charleston
Suite 2-352
Las Vegas
Nevada
89117
shellybarnum@
lvcm.com

5160 Las Vegas Boulevard South Las Vegas, Nevada 89119 www.wolfgangpuck.com

Gibbons Lane Winery LLC
P.O. Box 7755
Olympia, WA 98507
360.264.8466
www.donedei.com

Client
Walters Golf and Wolfgang Puck
Design Firm
**Ripple Strategic Design
& Consulting**
Designers
Raymond Perez, Dan McElhattan III

Client
Carolyn Lakewold, Gibbons Lane Winery
Design Firm
Hansen Design Company
Designers
Pat Hansen, Jacqueline Smith

Client
Red Canoe
Design Firm
Red Canoe
Art Director
Deb Koch
Designer
Caroline Kavanagh

red
cAnoe

347 CLEAR CREEK TRAIL
DEER LODGE, TN 37726
T 423.965.2223
F 423.965.1005
E STUDIO@REDCANOE.COM
www.redcanoe.com

Client
The Advantage Group, Pez Lake
Design Firm
Levine & Associates
Designer
Lena Markley

PEZ LAKE DEVELOPMENT LLC

5786 State Route 96 | Romulus, New York 14541

tel 607-869-5798 | fax 607-869-3329 | www.pezlake.com

Hillis**design**
PACKAGE DESIGN • BRAND IDENTITY

18326 Minnetonka Blvd.
Wayzata, MN 55391
(P) 952.404.9318
(F) 952.476.2943
www.hillisdesign.com

Client
Hillis Design
Design Firm
Hillis Design
Designer
Anna Clark

Cater First

7311 GEORGIA AVENUE, NW • WASHINGTON, DC 20012 • TEL 202.723.7900 • FAX 202.723.7033
www.cater first.com

Client
  Reilly Electric Company
Design Firm
  Dula Image Group
Art Director
  Melissa Luther
Designer
  Michael Dula

Repairs, Voice & Data Wiring
309654
A ANA, CALIFORNIA 92705
FAX (714) 731-0303

Client
  Cater First
Design Firm
  Levine & Associates
Designer
  Monica Snellings

RECORDINGS

P.O. Box 60129
Dayton, OH 45406

urbansociety1@aol.com

RECORDINGS

Client
  Urban Society Recordings
Design Firm
  **Anise V. Simpson
  Graphic Designer/Illustrator**
Designer
  Anise V. Simpson

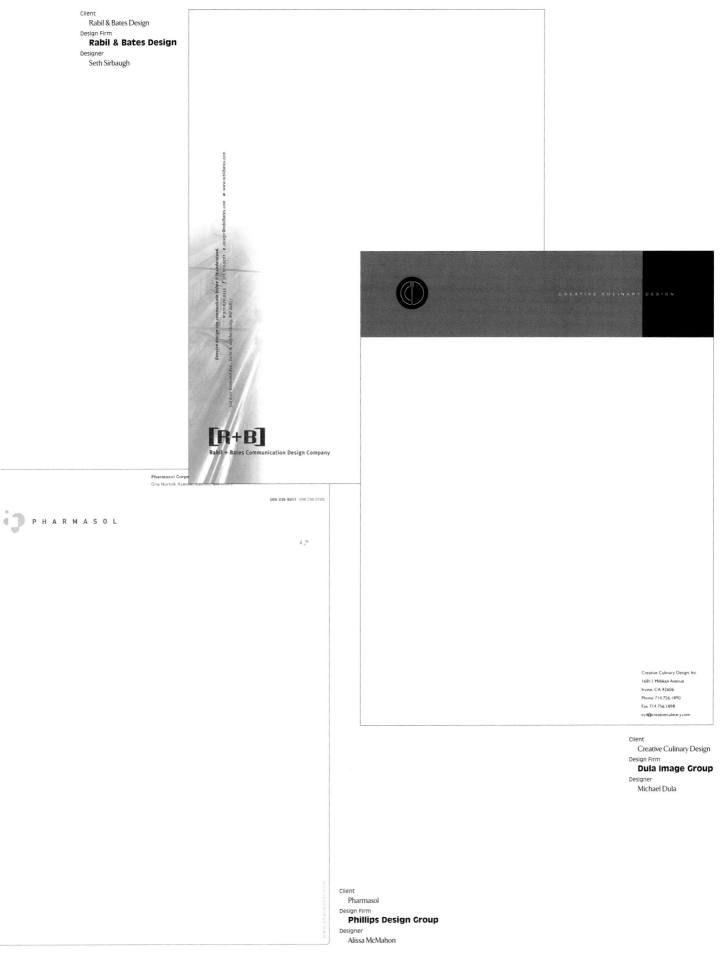

Client
Rabil & Bates Design
Design Firm
Rabil & Bates Design
Designer
Seth Sirbaugh

Genuine design can communicate before it is understood.
312 East Diamond Ave., Suite A, Gaithersburg, MD 20877
v 301.670.9355 **f** 301.670.9781 **e** design@rabilbates.com **w** www.rabilbates.com

[R+B]
Rabil + Bates Communication Design Company

CREATIVE CULINARY DESIGN

Pharmasol Corp
One Norfolk Avenue, Easton, MA 01915

508 238 8501 508 238 0105

PHARMASOL

Creative Culinary Design, Inc.
16811 Millikan Avenue
Irvine, CA 92606
Phone 714.756.1890
Fax 714.756.1898
ccd@creativeculinary.com

Client
Creative Culinary Design
Design Firm
Dula Image Group
Designer
Michael Dula

Client
Pharmasol
Design Firm
Phillips Design Group
Designer
Alissa McMahon

www.pharmasol.com

Client
  Aloha Restaurants, Inc.
Design Firm
  Dula Image Group
Designer
  Michael Dula

Client
  QSR Concepts Inc.
Design Firm
  Dula Image Group
Designer
  Michael Dula

Client
  Quadrant Health Strategies Inc.
Design Firm
  Sasaki Associates Inc.
Designers
  Kris Waldman, Zachary Siswick

Client
Hanford ARC
Design Firm
Buttitta Design
Designer
Patti Buttitta

23195 MAFFEI ROAD
SONOMA, CA 95476
TEL: 707 996 6633
FAX: 707 996 6641
LICENSE NO. 461167

123 University Place • Pittsburgh, Pennsylvania 15213 • 412.687.3876 • Fax 412.687.3877
www.netbeyond.net

Client
Net Beyond Communications
Design Firm
Elias/Savion Advertising
Designers
Ronnie Savion, Steve Baksis

Client
Rule 29
Design Firm
Rule 29
Designers
Justin Ahrens, Jim Boborci

R 29

Offset Atlanta
QUALITY COMMERCIAL PRINTING

1207 THRUN DRIVE | BATAVIA, IL 60510
P **630.482.9900** F 630.482.9909 W www.lighthousemktg.com

Client
Lighthouse Marketing Services, Inc.
Design Firm
Rule 29
Designers
Justin Ahrens, Jim Boborci

Offset Atlanta, Inc.
6659-G Peachtree Industrial Blvd.
Norcross, Georgia 30092
Phone: 770 448-2765
Fax: 770 448-2769
Web Site: www.offsetatlanta.com

Client
Offset Atlanta
Design Firm
WorldSTAR Design
Designer
Greg Guhl

Client
Interactive Sites
Design Firm
Rule 29
Designers
Justin Ahrens, Jim Boborci

INTERACTIVESITES

14988 North 78th Way
Second Floor
Scottsdale, Arizona 85260
www.interactivesites.com
480 707 1600
480 707 1601

WAINWRIGHT
INVESTMENT
COUNSEL, LLC

ONE BOSTON PLACE
BOSTON, MA 02108

TEL: 617.788.9900
FAX: 617.788.9740

WINVCOUNSEL.COM

Client
Wainwright Investment Counsel
Design Firm
Richland Design Associates
Designers
Judith Richland, Cynthia Zoppa

SHUTTER HONKEY STUDIO

CHRIS GRAY   2948 WEST SWAN DRIVE   SPRINGFIELD, MO 65807   417 886 0525

Client
Chris Gray
Design Firm
Prejean LoBue
Designers
Kevin Prejean, Gary LoBue, Jr.

Client
Commotion Promotions
Design Firm
Leibowitz Communications
Art Director, Designer
Rick Bargmann

Client
Inventing Flight
Design Firm
Graphica
Designers
Drew Cronenwett, Mollee Gray

1152 West Third Street

Dayton, Ohio 45407

937-222-0065

inventingflight.com

76 TRENTON AVENUE
EAST ATLANTIC BEACH, NY 11561
P +1 516.431.2651

THE CENTEN

p 415.543.3837
f 888.532.6197
www.prime-image.com

275 Fifth Street
San Francisco
California 94103

Client
Prime Image Media Group
Design Firm
Strongrrl
Designer
Julie R. Wheeler

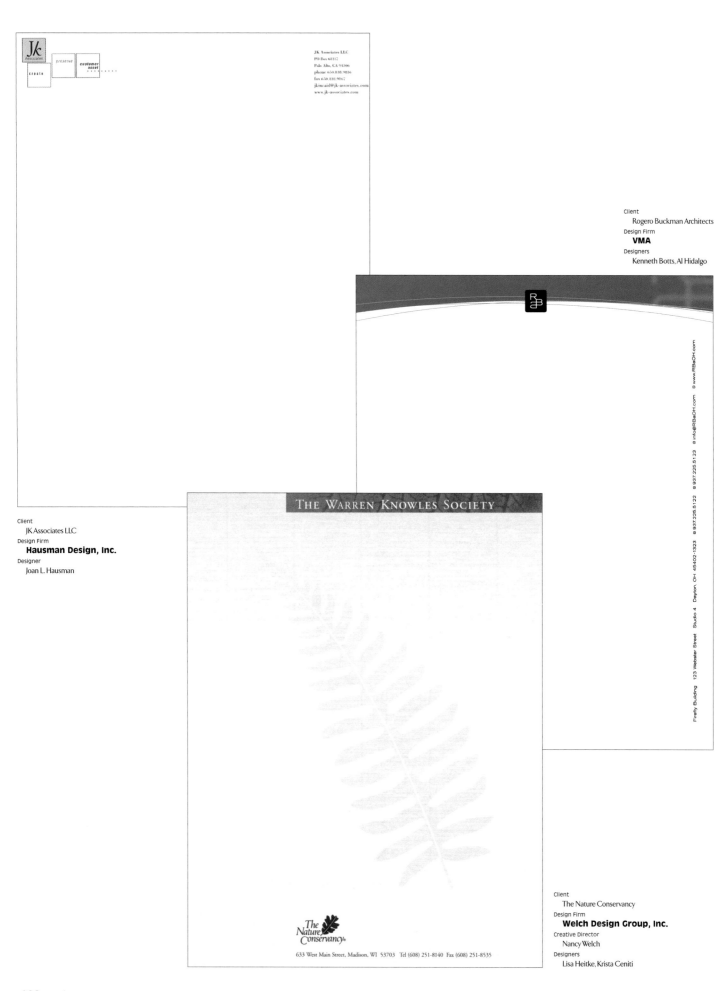

JK Associates LLC
PO Box 61117
Palo Alto, CA 94306
phone 650.838.9816
fax 650.838.9867
jkmcaid@jk-associates.com
www.jk-associates.com

Client
Rogero Buckman Architects
Design Firm
VMA
Designers
Kenneth Botts, Al Hidalgo

Client
JK Associates LLC
Design Firm
Hausman Design, Inc.
Designer
Joan L. Hausman

THE WARREN KNOWLES SOCIETY

The
Nature
Conservancy®

633 West Main Street, Madison, WI 53703   Tel (608) 251-8140   Fax (608) 251-8535

Firefly Building   123 Webster Street   Studio 4   Dayton, OH 45402-1323   @ 937.225.5122   @ 937.225.5123   @ info@RBaOH.com   @ www.RBaOH.com

Client
The Nature Conservancy
Design Firm
Welch Design Group, Inc.
Creative Director
Nancy Welch
Designers
Lisa Heitke, Krista Ceniti

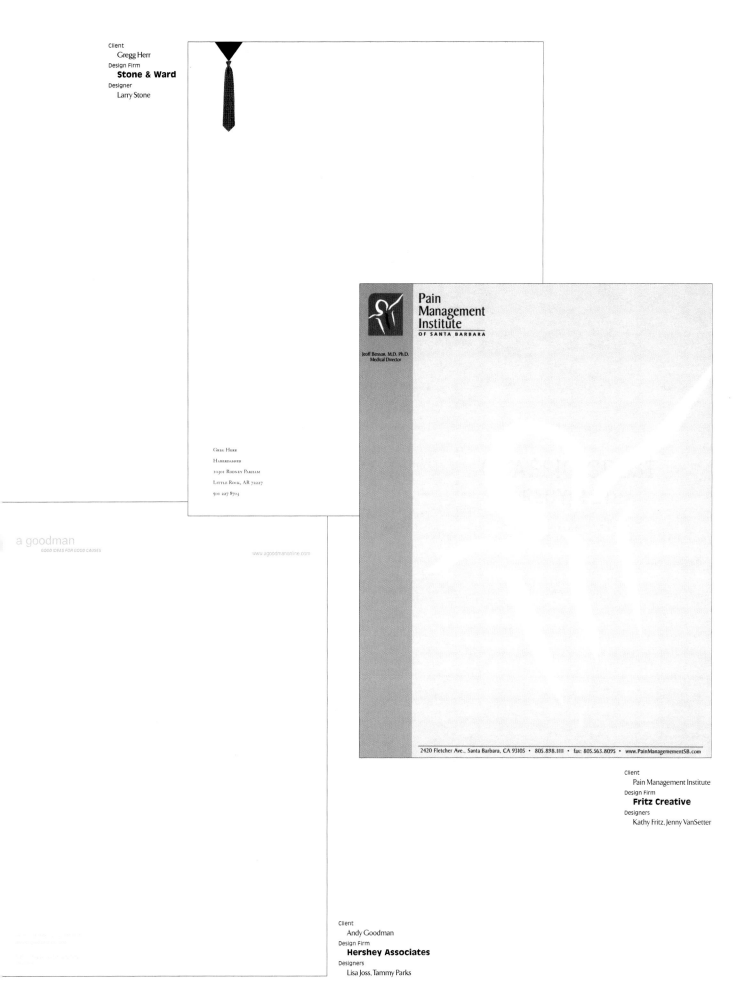

Client
Gregg Herr
Design Firm
Stone & Ward
Designer
Larry Stone

GREGG HERR
HABERDASHER
10301 RODNEY PARHAM
LITTLE ROCK, AR 72227

501 227 8703

a goodman
GOOD IDEAS FOR GOOD CAUSES

www.agoodmanonline.com

Pain
Management
Institute
OF SANTA BARBARA

Jeoff Benson, M.D., Ph.D.
Medical Director

2420 Fletcher Ave., Santa Barbara, CA 93105 • 805.898.1111 • fax: 805.563.8095 • www.PainManagementSB.com

Client
Pain Management Institute
Design Firm
Fritz Creative
Designers
Kathy Fritz, Jenny VanSetter

Client
Andy Goodman
Design Firm
Hershey Associates
Designers
Lisa Joss, Tammy Parks

Client
  Lightwave Systems
Design Firm
  Fritz Creative
Designer
  Kathy Fritz

LIGHT**WAVE**
SYSTEMS

16   fax: 805.684.6696   www.lightwave-systems.com

Ogilvy Hill
INSURANCE

Client
  Ogilvy Hill Insurance
Design Firm
  Fritz Creative
Designers
  Kathy Fritz, Wendy Windholtz

Tufton
Sports &
  Management west

Client
  Tufton Sports & Management West
Design Firm
  Planit
Designer
  Molly Stevenson

7349 VIA PASEO DEL SUR • SCOTTSDALE, AZ 85258
PHONE: (480) 368-9854 • FAX: (480) 368-9952
www.ripkenbaseball.com

Tufton
Sports &
  Management
Baltimore, Mar
410-823-0808

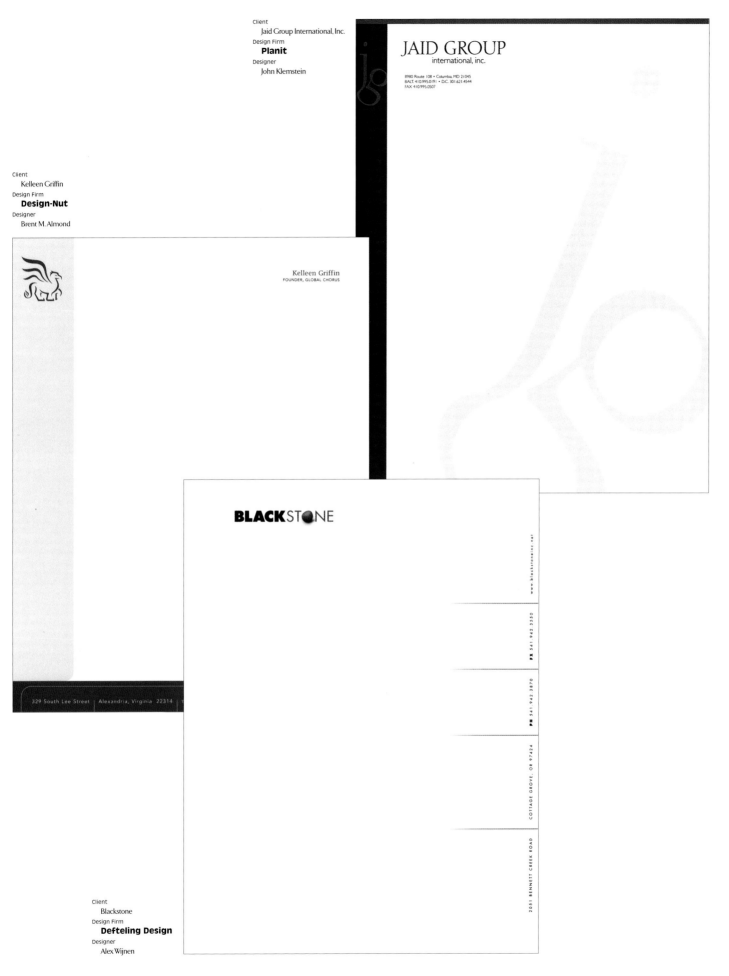

Client
Jaid Group International, Inc.
Design Firm
Planit
Designer
John Klemstein

Client
Kelleen Griffin
Design Firm
Design-Nut
Designer
Brent M. Almond

Client
Blackstone
Design Firm
Defteling Design
Designer
Alex Wijnen

PLANIT
integrated brand communications

The Power Plant
601 East Pratt Street
Baltimore, Maryland 21202

T 410.962.8500
F 410.962.8508
I www.planitagency.com

info@biancomarchilonis.com
60 Dedham Ave.
Needham, MA 02492-3061
T: 781-444-9077 F: 781-444-8016

BiancoMarchilonis**Design**
Turning concepts into solutions.

Client
Bianco Marchilonis Design
Design Firm
Bianco Marchilonis Design
Designers
Peter Bianco, Karen Marchilonis

Client
Planit
Design Firm
Planit
Designers
Molly Stevenson, Ed Callahan

OEM LABELING SYSTEMS
Ingenious solutions for pressure sensitive applications

934 Salem Parkway
PO Box 830
Salem OH 44460-0830

(330) 332-8596
fax (330) 332-8598

www.oemlabeling.com
info@oemlabeling.com

Client
OEM Labeling System
Design Firm
Crawford Design
Designer
Alison Crawford

Client
GYMR
Design Firm
Smarteam Communications, Inc.
Designers
Brent Almond, Andrew Marciniak

Strategic and Creative Communications

GYMR · Garrett, Yu Hussein
McCabe & Reis, LLC

1825 Connecticut Ave., NW | Suite 650 | Washington,

IAAPA

International
Association of
Amusement Parks
and Attractions

1448 Duke Street
Alexandria, VA 22314 USA
703.836.4800
www.iaapa.org
iaapa@iaapa.org

Fax Numbers

Communications
703.836.3036

Membership
703.836.1192

Convention,
Government Relations,
President
703.836.4801

Finance, Training,
Computer Operations
703.836.6742

Publications
703.836.2824

Fax-on-demand
703.836.9678

Client
International Association of
Amusement Parks and Attractions
Design Firm
Kircher
Designer
Bruce E. Morgan

h² k
design

tel 360.939.2085
fax 360.939.2095

p.o. box 1270
10031 sr 532, suite b
stanwood, wa 98292

h2kdesign.com

Design Firm
Monster Design

Client
Freerein
Design Firm
**Hornall Anderson
Design Works**
Designers
Jack Anderson, Mark Popich, Tobi
Brown, Steffanie Lorig, Bruce Stigler,
Elmer dela Cruz, John Anderle,
Gretchen Cook

freerein   www.freerein.com

JEFFRY POND ARCHITECT INC

JP

450 HARRISON AVENUE . SUITE 224 . BOSTON MA 02118 . TELEPHONE 617.482.0339 . TELEFAX 617.482.0376 . EMAIL pondarch@aol.com

Client
Jeffry Pond
Design Firm
Nassar Design
Designer
Nélida Nassar

Client
   Box USA
Design Firm
   Connelly Design, Inc.
Creative Director
   Susan Graim
Designer
   Kate Brankin

BOX USA

2100 Sanders Road, Ste. 200
Northbrook, IL 60062-6141
847.790.2800
www.boxusa.com

Client
   Aue Design Studio
Design Firm
   Aue Design Studio
Art Director
   Mary Ann Aue
Designer
   Jen Aue

aue design studio
278 east garfield road
aurora, oh 44202

p 330 995 0014

f 330 995 0054
www.auedesignstudio.com

Think Big ... Act Small™

COMMUNICATION DESIGN FOR MARKETING

M

MERTEN
DESIGN
GROUP

1885 South Pearl Street • Denver, CO • 80210 | 303.282.5580 • fax 282.1636
e.mail bam@mertendesign.com • www.mertendesign.com

Client
   Merten Design Group
Design Firm
   Merten Design Group
Designer
   Barry Merten

the corner office

commercial interiors

343 East 5th Street, Dayton Ohio 45402
v) 937.222.02

Client
    The Corner Office
Design Firm
    The Marketing Formula
Art Director, Designer
    Errin Hahn

Client
    iRefinery
Design Firm
    Rise Agency
Creative Director
    A.C. Bulluck

http://www.digitalvisioneers.com

One Union Square West
    New York, New York 10003
    Phone 212.691.6051
                Fax 646.336.9023

I REFINERY

PRINTRICATE

the machinery of ideas

One Union Square West, New York, NY 10003 P. 212.691.6051 F. 646.336.9023

www.printricate.com

Client
    Printricate
Design Firm
    Rise Agency
Creative Director
    A.C. Bulluck

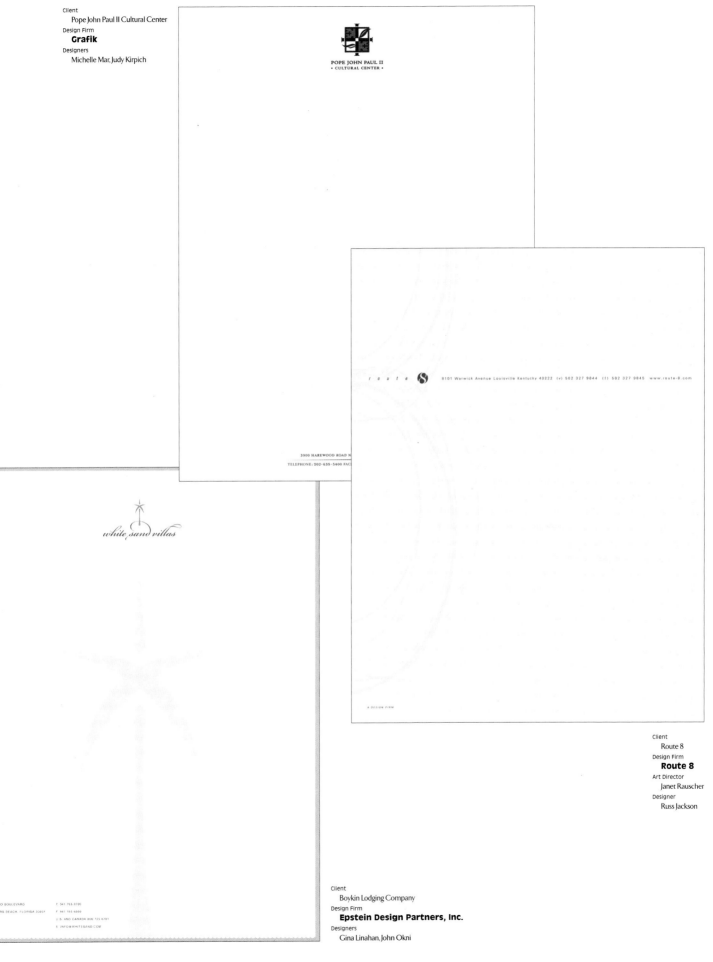

POPE JOHN PAUL II
· CULTURAL CENTER ·

3900 HAREWOOD ROAD N
TELEPHONE: 202-635-5400 FAC

route **8**   8101 Warwick Avenue Louisville Kentucky 40222 (v) 502 327 9844 (f) 502 327 9845 www.route-8.com

A DESIGN FIRM

white sand villas

@TERO BOULEVARD
MYERS BEACH, FLORIDA 33931
U.S. AND CANADA
E INFO@WHITESAND.COM

T. 941.765.X700
F. 941 765 6999
800 725 X701

Client
Fifth Letter
Design Firm
Fifth Letter
Designer
Elliot Strunk

Client
Richard Zeid Design
Design Firm
Richard Zeid Design
Designer
Richard Zeid

Client
The Cleveland Institute of Art
Design Firm
Epstein Design Partners, Inc.
Designer
Karen Myers

Client
Tom Fowler, Inc.
Design Firm
Tom Fowler, Inc.
Designer
Thomas G. Fowler

Tom Fowler, Inc.
Graphic Communicators

111 Westport Avenue
Norwalk, Connecticut 06851
T: 203-845-0700
F: 203-847-1169
E: MAIL@TOMFOWLERINC.COM
W: TOMFOWLERINC.COM

Client
Catapult Advisors
Design Firm
ProWolfe Partners, Inc.
Art Director
Doug Wolfe
Designer
Justin Johnson

CATAPULT
Strategy in Action

Catapult Advisors, LLC
Suite 1400
7777 Bonhomme Avenue
St. Louis, Missouri 63105

T: 314.361.2448
F: 314.361.6146
www.catapult-advisors.com

Audio and   Web: www.cpcircle.com

Music for

All Media

657 Big Timber Dr.

Joliet, Illinois 60431

Tel: 815.730.8705

Fax: 815.730.3672   E-Mail: info@www.cpcircle.com

Client
Chicago Producers Circle
Design Firm
Bullet Communications, Inc.
Designer
Timothy Scott Kump

Beaulieu Vineyard.
LE CORPS de Latour

POST OFFICE BOX 534 · RUTHERFORD, CA 94573
TELEPHONE 800 373 5896 · FACSIMILE 707 967 0558
WWW.BVWINE.COM

Client
Beaulieu Vineyard le Corps de Latour
Design Firm
Halleck
Designer
Wayne Wright

Client
Sherman College of
Straight Chiropractic
Design Firm
Set?Communicate!
Designers
Steve Thomas, Dan Wold

SHERMAN
COLLEGE
of STRAIGHT
CHIROPRACTIC

W W W . S H E R M A N . E D U
2 . SPARTANBURG. SOUTH CAROLINA 29304

TXS Industrial Design

TXS Industrial Design, Inc.   1761 International Parkway, #135 Richardson Texas 75081   p 972.783.2798   www.txsdesign.com
f 972.783.9722

Client
TXS Industrial Design
Design Firm
TXS Industrial Design
Designers
Tim Terleski, Staci Mininger

An
Emerging
Episcopal
Congregation

www.churchbeloved.org
115 West Seventh Street
Charlotte, NC 28202
✝
704-342-3114
704-332-7747 fax
704-575-0097 mobile

3518 Third Avenue

San Diego, California 92103

Telephone: 619 298 2834

Facsimile: 619 298 4143

egmail@theexpressgroup.com

www.theexpressgroup.com

Silver Bridge Tours • 218-B East Tremont Ave. • Charlotte, NC 28203 • phone: (704) 358-1715 • toll-free: (877) 917-1715 • fax (704) 358-8350

silverbridgetours.com

PReJean LoBue
CREATIVE WORKS

ADVERTISING, DESIGN, CORPORATE IDENTITY & BRANDING, ANNUAL
REPORTS, STRATEGIC THINKING, NEW MEDIA, VISUAL ICONS, WEB DESIGN
PRINT COMMUNICATIONS, PACKAGE DESIGN & OTHER CREATIVE THINGS

SAINT CLAIR PRESS

siana 70508   337.593.9051 voice   337.593.9053 fax

1203 E. St Clair Street | Indianapolis, IN 46202 | PH 317.612.9100 | TF 800.748.0323 | FX 317.638.6793

Jefferson
AT BAY MEADOWS

1101 PARK PLACE • SAN MATEO, CA 94403
PHONE 650 581 3700 • FAX 650 581 3680
www.jeffersonatbaymeadows.com

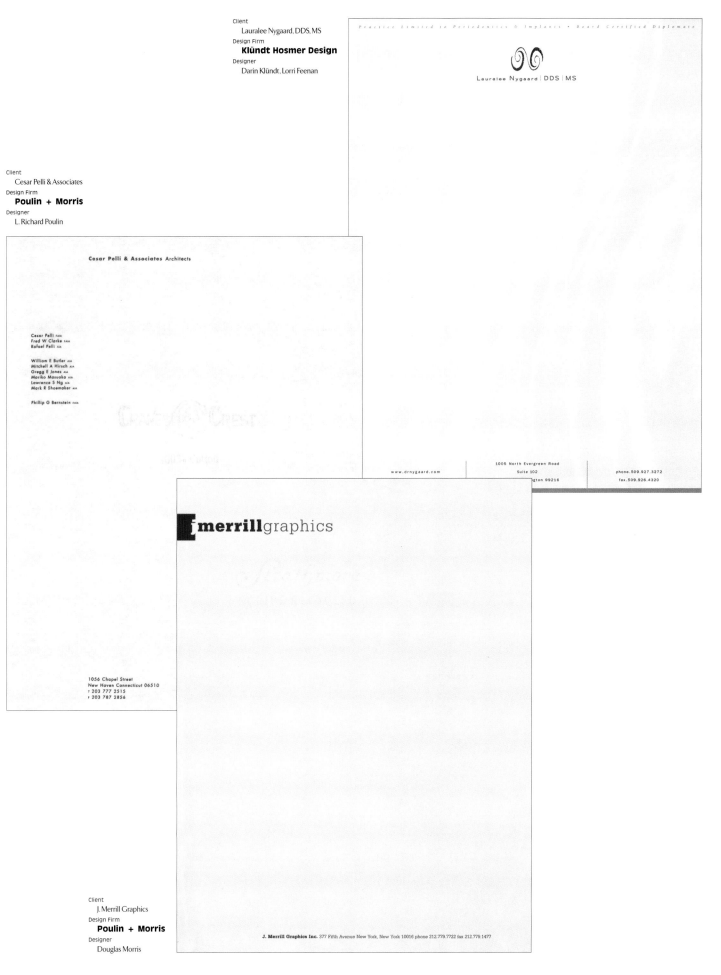

Client
Lauralee Nygaard, DDS, MS
Design Firm
Klündt Hosmer Design
Designer
Darin Klündt, Lorri Feenan

Client
Cesar Pelli & Associates
Design Firm
Poulin + Morris
Designer
L. Richard Poulin

Client
J. Merrill Graphics
Design Firm
Poulin + Morris
Designer
Douglas Morris

Laclede Capital LLC
7733 Forsyth Blvd. 11th Fl
St. Louis, Missouri 63105

LACLEDE CAPITAL

Telephone: 314.862.9009
Facsimile: 314.862.5556
www.lacledecapital.com

INVESTMENT BANKING / FINANCIAL CONSULTING
Securities offered through Capital West Securities, Inc. Member NASD and SIPC.

Client
  Laclede Capital
Design Firm
  ProWolfe Partners
Art Director
  Doug Wolfe
Designer
  Justin Johnson

2345 kettner blvd
san diego, ca 92101

p. 619 234 6631
f. 619 234 1807

www.miresbrands.com

mires > design for brands™

Client
  Mires
Design Firm
  Mires
Creative Director
  John Ball
Designer
  Miguel Perez

CORPORATE IDENTITY MANUALS

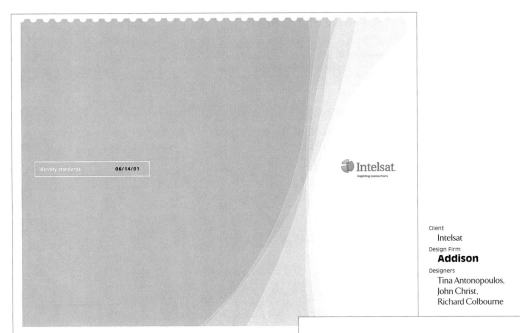

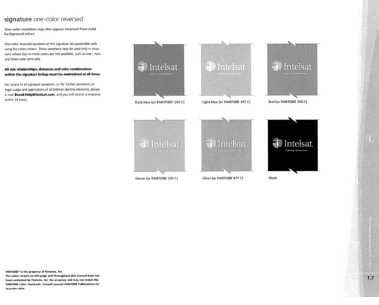

Client
Intelsat
Design Firm
Addison
Designers
Tina Antonopoulos,
John Christ,
Richard Colbourne

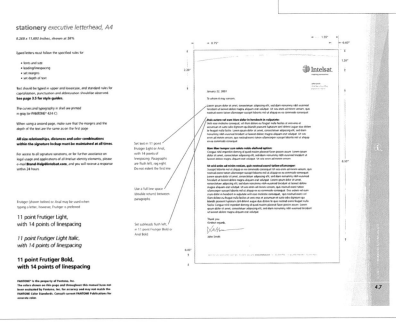

VISUAL IDENTITY GUIDELINES

A MANUAL TO HELP YOU
BUILD A STRONG BRAND

Client
Ryan Company
Design Firm
Tilka Design
Designer
Sarah Steil

SEPTEMBER 2001

Control Area

POSITIVE, 2-COLOR LOGO

Shape

Wordmark

Color Bar

Tagline

REVERSE, 2-COLOR LOGO IN SHAPE

POSITIVE, 1-COLOR LOGO

REVERSE, 1-COLOR LOGO IN SHAPE

LOGO COMPONENTS

The Ryan logo is always comprised of the following three elements: wordmark, color bar, and tagline. Sometimes a boxed shape contains these elements.

Wordmark

The wordmark is the distinctive typographic treatment of "Ryan" with the shamrock in the center of the "R." Do not separate the shamrock from the wordmark or use it as a separate element. The color of the shamrock is dark green, black, or white in all circumstances.

Color Bar

The color bar underscores our company name and places the name on a horizontal line. It adds style, strengthens our brand color, and gives emphasis and attention to our name.

Ryan Tagline

When the "Building Lasting Relationships" tagline appears with our logo, it is in a distinctive font and always in the same position. In body text, the tagline is set with initial caps in the same font and style as the surrounding text.

Shape

The dark green shape is used in some marketing applications and reinforces the strength of our visual identity. Its size and relationship to the wordmark always remain consistent.

Size

On most standard business applications, the width of the wordmark is 1.125". The width of the shape is 1.5". When used larger, the size is increased in 25 percent increments.

Color

Our brand color is green. The wordmark and tagline appear either in dark green or white. The color bar appears in the lighter green.

Placement

The logo generally appears on the right side of any given format, whether on the top or bottom.

Control Area

When using the positive version of the visual identity, the control area is a defined area maintained around the logo. No other visual elements are to appear within this area.

Please note: Do not add art, such as clip art, to the logo or within the control area and/or boxed shape surrounding the wordmark.

SYSTEM ELEMENTS   5   *Logo*

SEPTEMBER 2001

TRADE SHOW EXHIBIT BOOTH, 10' X 10'

TRADE SHOW EXHIBIT BOOTH, 10' X 20'

TABLE TOP EXHIBIT

SIGNAGE   25   *Trade Show Exhibit Booth*

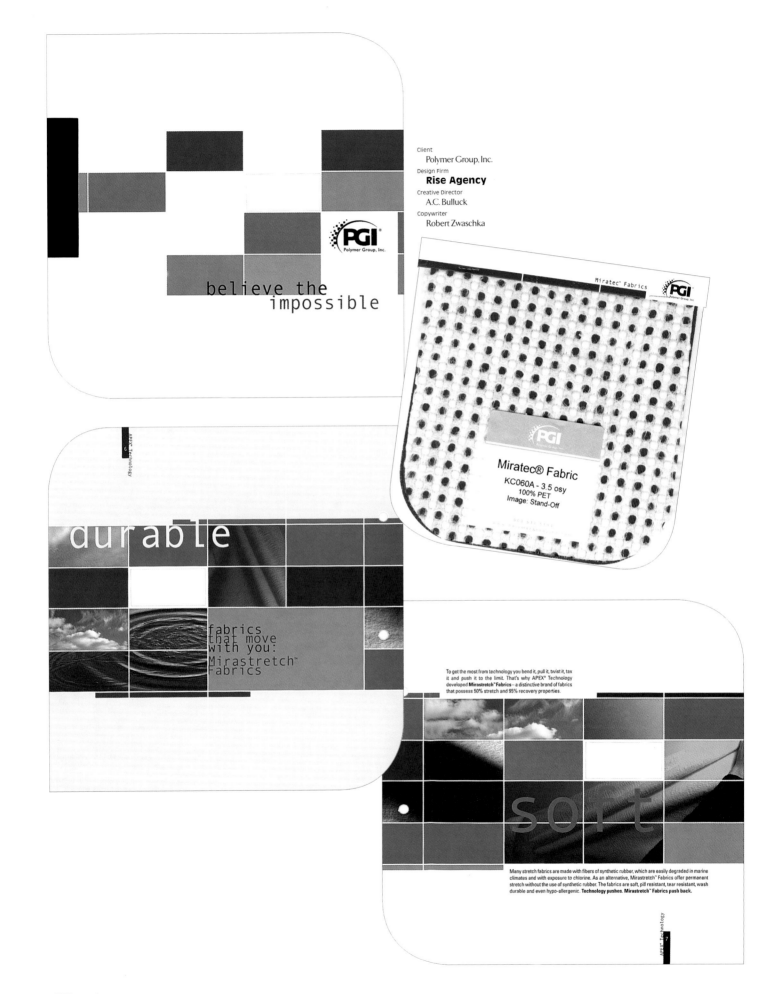

believe the
impossible

Client
Polymer Group, Inc.
Design Firm
Rise Agency
Creative Director
A.C. Bulluck
Copywriter
Robert Zwaschka

Miratec® Fabrics

Miratec® Fabric

KC060A - 3.5 osy
100% PET
Image: Stand-Off

durable

fabrics
that move
with you:
Mirastretch™
Fabrics

APEX Technology

To get the most from technology you bend it, pull it, twist it, tax it and push it to the limit. That's why APEX® Technology developed **Mirastretch™ Fabrics**—a distinctive brand of fabrics that possess 50% stretch and 95% recovery properties.

soft

Many stretch fabrics are made with fibers of synthetic rubber, which are easily degraded in marine climates and with exposure to chlorine. As an alternative, Mirastretch™ Fabrics offer permanent stretch without the use of synthetic rubber. The fabrics are soft, pill resistant, tear resistant, wash durable and even hypo-allergenic. **Technology pushes. Mirastretch™ Fabrics push back.**

APEX Technology 7

A Diageo Company

Color Presentation on Black Background for Television and Video Presentations Only:

In television and video production, the color presentation of the BURGER KING Bun Halves and Crescent Logo appears over a field of black. The "Highlights" in the BURGER KING Bun Halves and Crescent Logo are white. BURGER KING BLUE matches PMS 293C, BURGER KING RED matches PMS 485C and BURGER KING YELLOW matches PMS 130C. For computer based presentations, see page 4-4.

When on black, the "Crescent" of the BURGER KING Bun Halves and Crescent Logo is PMS 293C and the "TM" is white. The "Highlights" on the "Bun Halves" are also white.

Color Presentation on Kraft Paper:

In print production on kraft paper, the color presentation of the BURGER KING Bun Halves and Crescent Logo appears as shown.

Spot Printing on Kraft Paper:

The presentation of the BURGER KING Bun Halves and Crescent Logo is three-color using the following approved colors:

BURGER KING BLUE- PANTONE 286U
BURGER KING RED- PANTONE 485U
BURGER KING YELLOW- PANTONE 129U

This is the only acceptable three-color use when spot printing on kraft paper.

Note: The Logo shown is for Illustration only. Printing on kraft paper may result in different color densities. Be sure to visually match colors to the approved color sample.

Client
Burger King

Design Firm
Atwater Creative

Slides and Electronic Presentations

The lead idea or key insight of chart, graphic or bullet points

Note the Source for current and future clarity

Identify Region/Market and Document Name

Alternate treatment for Lead Idea slide with two-lined title.

Sub-titles: Arial Italic, 26 point
Column titles: Arial Bold, 24 point
Chart text: Arial Bold, 23 point and Arial Regular, 20 point
Bottom text: Arial Regular, 12 point
All text upper and lower case
Letterspacing: Normal
Type alignment: Titles and sub-titles: Left align. Other text centered in main content area below subtitle, above bottom text and inside margins

4-4

Client
Anacomp

Design Firm
Mires

Creative Director
John Ball

Designer
Deborah Hom

Illustrator
Miguel Perez

Copywriter
Danniel White

5.

Applications
The Anacomp logo can be applied to virtually any surface for a wide variety of communications and promotional uses. The corporate style guidelines should be observed in all applications.

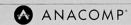

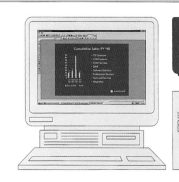

The following color palette is used when creating Manulife College Savings materials.

Color Swatch	Pantone Uncoated	Pantone Coated	CMYK 4-Color		RGB Web		Usage
Dark Green	PMS 349 U	PMS 626 C	C 85 / M 0 / Y 85 / K 35		R 0 / G 102 / B 51	# 006633	> Manulife logo only
Dark Blue	PMS 547 U	PMS 547 C	C 94 / M 24 / Y 0 / K 76		R 0 / G 51 / B 102	# 003366	> Primary color blocks / > Headline text / > Subhead text / > Accent squares
Dark Orange	PMS 159 U	PMS 159 C	C 10 / M 70 / Y 100 / K 0		R 204 / G 102 / B 0	# CC6600	> Subhead text / > Accent text / > Accent squares
Beige	PMS 468 U	PMS 468 C	C 0 / M 3 / Y 15 / K 3		R 255 / G 255 / B 204	# FFFFCC	> Color blocks/strips
Medium Gray	PMS Warm Gray 5 U	PMS Warm Gray 5 C	C 0 / M 5 / Y 10 / K 20		R 153 / G 153 / B 153	# 999999	> Color blocks/strips / > Accent rules / > Caption text
Bright Green	PMS 390 U	PMS 390 C	C 30 / M 0 / Y 100 / K 10		R 153 / G 203 / B 102	# 99CC66	> Accent squares / > Support graphics
Slate Green	PMS 624 U	PMS 624 C	C 35 / M 0 / Y 20 / K 10		R 102 / G 153 / B 153	# 669999	> Color blocks / > Accent squares / > Support graphics
Slate Blue	PMS 5425 U	PMS 5425 C	C 25 / M 0 / Y 0 / K 25		R 153 / G 153 / B 204	# 9999CC	> Color blocks / > Accent squares / > Support graphics
Maroon	PMS 201 U	PMS 202 C	C 30 / M 80 / Y 60 / K 0		R 153 / G 0 / B 0	# 990000	> Accent squares / > Support graphics
Light Orange	PMS 138 U	PMS 138 C	C 10 / M 50 / Y 100 / K 0		R 255 / G 153 / B 0	# FF9900	> Accent squares / > Support graphics
Yellow	PMS 129 U	PMS 130 C	C 0 / M 20 / Y 100 / K 0		R 255 / G 204 / B 51	# FFCC33	> Accent squares / > Support graphics

Client
Manulife College Savings
Design Firm
RainCastle Communications
Designer
Tony Catlin

---

10. Proofreader's Checklist

The following is a checklist for proofreaders to make sure certain information appears on MCS collateral:

☐ Product Number (xxx)
MonthYear-529xxx

☐ Web Address
www.manulifecollegesavings.com

☐ Phone Number
1-866-MANU529 (1-866-626-8529)

☐ Legal Copy
When referring to Manulife College Savings only use this copy:

Manulife College Savings is being distributed by ManEquity, Inc., managed by T. Rowe Price and sponsored by the Alaska Trust. ManEquity, Inc. is a member of the NASD and is listed with the Municipal Securities Rulemaking Board (MSRB). Any contract distributed on or after January 1, 2002, subject to regulatory approval, will be distributed by Manulife Financial Securities LLC, the successor broker/dealer to ManEquity, Inc.

Manulife Financial and the block design are registered service marks and trademarks of The Manufacturers Life Insurance Company and are used by it and its affiliates including Manulife Financial Corporation.

When referring to Manulife College Savings and Manulife Wood Logan use this copy:

Manulife College Savings is being distributed by ManEquity, Inc., or other broker/dealers appointed by ManEquity, Inc., managed by T. Rowe Price and sponsored by the Alaska Trust. ManEquity, Inc. is a member of the NASD and is listed with the Municipal Securities Rulemaking Board (MSRB). Any contract distributed on or after January 1, 2002, subject to regulatory approval, will be distributed by Manulife Financial Securities LLC, the successor broker/dealer to ManEquity, Inc.

Manulife Financial and the block design are registered service marks and trademarks of The Manufacturers Life Insurance Company and are used by it and its affiliates including Manulife Financial Corporation.

☐ FDIC Information: For pieces intended for the public/consumer only.
529 Plans are not FDIC insured, may lose value and are not bank or state guaranteed.
(9 point Frutiger 45 Light light is used, surrounded by a .5 point rule.)

☐ Copyright Information
© (year). All rights reserved. Information included in this material is believed to be accurate as of the (month) (year) printing date.
(copyright sentence should be used when necessary, using 5.5 point Frutiger 45 Light.)

☐ Taglines
"A National Plan Sponsored by the Alaska Trust" is used for insert sheets and pre-printed shells.

"The Multi-Managed Way to Save For College" is used as an alternate tagline.

☐ Fund Names
> A I M Advisors, Inc.
> Davis Advisors
> MFS Investment Management
> OppenheimerFunds, Inc.
> Pacific Investment Management Company (PIMCO)
> Templeton Global Advisors, Limited
> T. Rowe Price Associates, Inc.

☐ Pie Chart Legal Disclaimers
Because risk tolerance is subjective, portfolio selection should only be made after you and your financial consultant have completed a full assessment of your total financial picture.

These represent target allocations only. For actual allocations, please visit our website at www.manulifecollegesavings.com under Portfolio Choices.

☐ Mailing Address
What address info is needed? Is Service Office, Boston Office, Stamford Office or other address info needed on the printed piece?

☐ Service Mark
A service mark (SM) should come after the tag line, "There is no greater gift than the gift of knowledge", wherever it appears." It should appear as follows: There is no greater gift than the gift of knowledge".

---

6. Graphic Elements

Consistent graphic style
To create a consistent brand, Manulife College Savings' graphic style utilizes the college campus painting in conjunction with large blocks of color from the established color palette. Thin gray or white vertical and horizontal lines are also used. Small squares of colors are used, in many cases, at intersections of lines.

Examples of existing collateral items will be shown to demonstrate how all of these elements can and should be used.

Usage of college campus illustration
The painting of the the college campus is the centerpiece of the Manulife College Savings plan. The colors in this painting work well with the color palette given in section 2.

In all cases, the illustration should be used in whole, or in pieces as demonstrated in existing pieces of collateral and the web site. See Figure 1.

Figure 1.

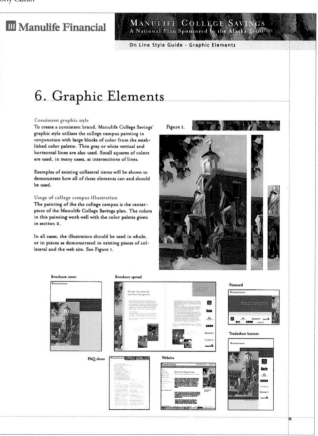

Brochure cover   Brochure spread   Postcard

FAQ sheet   Website   Tradeshow banner

Client
Relizon

Design Firm
Graphica

Designers
Melissa Sass,
Kathy Hemming.
Jeff Stapleton

THE HYOGO SHINKIN BANK, LTD.

Client
Hyogo Shinkin Bank
Design Firm
Cymbic
Creative Director
Kenichi Nishiwaki
Designer
Ken Kubo

1.0   INTRODUCTION

Purpose
The purpose of this Graphic Identity Guideline
is to document basic graphic components and
their applications. It is not intended to be used
for fabrication but to recommend a basic
guideline for identity placements and usage.

Identity Concept
Future - "Mirai"
The contemporary and technological
expression of the "wild Chrysanthemum" with
arched dots suggests Hyoshin's continuous
commitment to grow with customers' needs.
It represents Hyoshin's leadership in providing
the right solutions for the customers' future.

このガイドラインの目的は、基本的なグラフィック
エレメンの説明とその使い方を示すものです。色々な
制作物を作る為、このガイドラインの各ページをその
ままま使って制作するのではなく、アイデンティティ・
イメージの配置の参考にしてください。

イメージ・コンセプト
フューチャー／未来
＜のじぎく＞をモダンかつハイテクな表現にしてみま
した。アーチ状になった点は、テクノロジーと
共にお客さまのニーズにお答えしながら、お客さまと
共に歩み続けていくという意慾を表しています。
又、お客さまの未来のために、ニーズにあった対応を
常に心がける強いリーダーシップ精神を表しています。

HYOSHIN

8.0   PACKAGING

Bag
Signature   White on any of Hyoshin colors

紙袋
シグネチャー   いずれかの高感カラーの地に白抜き
のシグネチャー

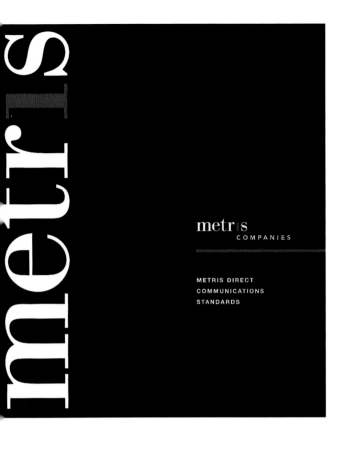

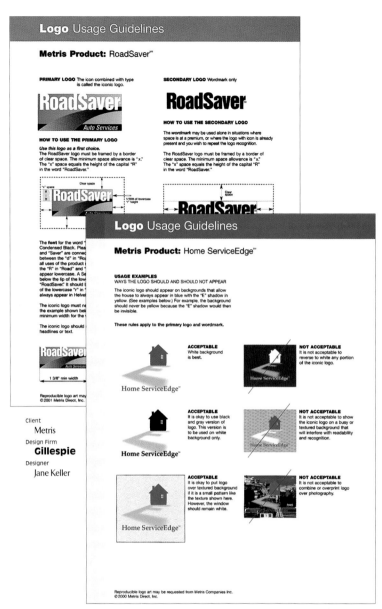

Client
Metris

Design Firm
Gillespie

Designer
Jane Keller

Client
AMD

Design Firm
FutureBrand HyperMedia

Designers
Carol Wolf, Tom Li

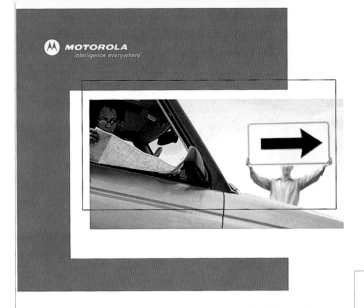

MOTOROLA DESIGN GUIDELINES
Version 1.0   October 2001

Multimedia Cover Slides

Multimedia Content Slides

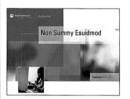

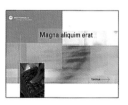

Motorola Design Guidelines   Version 1.0   October 2001

Print External Newsletter Cover

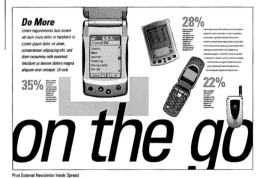

Print External Newsletter Inside Spread

Motorola Design Guidelines   Version 1.0   October 2001

Client
   Motorola
Design Firm
   Graphica
Designers
   Melissa Sass, Judy Smith,
   Kathy Hemming, Mark Stockstill,
   Jeff Stapleton, Beth Johnson,
   Cindy Schnell, Greg Simmons,
   Susan Dorenkemper

PLAUT

Plaut AG
Corporate Identity & Branding

Graphic Guidelines & Standards

Version 2:
02 July 2001

Global Launch
01 Oct 2001

©2001 Plaut

Gill Fishman Associates, Inc.
gfa@gillfishmandesign.com

955 Massachusetts Avenue   Cambridge, MA 02139   USA
Tel 617.492.5666   Fax 617.547.2501

Client
Plaut Consulting
Design Firm
Gill Fishman Associates
Creative Director
Gill Fishman
Designer
Jenn Jacobs

A. 1 COLOR REVERSED OUT USE:
This use is allowed only when Plaut name recognition must be shown on non-Plaut materials
such as partnership brochures w/ dark color fields and Power Point presentations.
Company Name and Global Brand Mark: Reversed out to all white
File Name: PLAUT_KO.eps

B. 2 COLOR REVERSED OUT USE:
This use is allowed only when Plaut name recognition must be shown on non-Plaut materials
such as partnership brochures and incentive materials w/ dark color fields.
Company Name: Plaut Yellow
Global Brand Mark: Reversed out to all white
File Name: PLAUT_KOtext.eps

---

46   **Incentive Program**

All items should be used to promote the Plaut signature,
not diminish its look. Always place in a position and color that
is appropriate and distinguished.

Black is the primary color used for the incentives program. Black was chosen
to help enhance the look of the logo as the yellow color appears best when
on black. Also, black is the most consistent color of all of the specified Plaut
colors from material to material.

Below are the recommended uses and file names
for the following items:

Mouse Pad   File Name: PLAUT_MOUSE.eps
Polo Shirt   File Name: PLAUT_POLO.eps
Canvas Laptop Bag   File Name: PLAUT_BAG.eps
Coffee Mug   File Name: PLAUT_MUG.eps
Name Tag   File Name: PLAUT_TAG.qrk

OTHER ACCEPTABLE BACKGROUND COLORS:

White
Silver Metallic
Plaut Yellow (ONLY if it matches 1225)

MOUSE PAD
Black mouse pad with 2 color logo (Mark in Plaut yellow,
Company Name in white), 40%K logo and Plaut URL.

EMBROIDERED POLO SHIRT
Black shirt with 2 color logo (Mark in Plaut yellow,
Company Name in white)

CANVAS LAPTOP BAG
Black bag with 2 color logo (Mark in Plaut yellow,
Company Name in white)

COFFEE MUGS
Black or Plaut yellow mug with 2 color logo on one side,
the Plaut tagline on the other.

SVEN KIELGAS
Chief Marketing and
Investor Relations Officer

PLAUT

NAME TAGS
Name and Title with 2 color logo

Plaut AG   Corporate Identity Standards   Version 2: 13 June 2001   Gill Fishman Associates, Inc.

Novell.
branding
guidelines

PROMOTIONAL VERTICAL BANNERS

PROMOTIONAL HORIZONTAL BANNERS

Novell
connecting
points

Novell
partner
solutions

Novell
connecting
points

Novell
Brainshare
2001

PROMOTIONAL FLAGS*

Novell
education
programs

CORPORATE
PACKAGING:
All packaging products
are accompanied by
an assortment of
standardized pieces.
Typical in-box components
include registration cards,
reference guides and
license agreements.

Product packaging is
always developed in
concert with Novell
Corporate Marketing
Communication and a
Product Operations
Manager.

PRODUCT BOX

Novell.
NetWare.

UPGRADE BOX

Novell. NetWare
Cluster Services
for NetWare 5

CD ENVELOPES

Novell
BorderManager

Novell
GroupWise

DOCUMENTATION

Novell
ZENworks 2
ManageWise 2.6

Novell.
NetWare

Novell

Novell Branding Guidelines

Client
Novell, Inc.
Design Firm
Hornall Anderson Design Works
Designers
Larry Anderson, Jack Anderson,
James Tee, Holly Craven,
Kaye Farmer, Jay Hilburn,
Belinda Bowling

GLOBAL BRANDING

SheaHomes
Caring since 1881

Client
Shea Homes

Design Firm
Gauger & Silva

Designer
Lori Murphy

LA VIGNE
SheaHomes

FALBROOKE
AT KRISTOPHER RANCH

SheaHomes

Community Entry Signage

The entry signage breaks from the use of the Shea Blue background to reflect the individual design style of the community. The only requirement is that the community logo include the Shea Homes logo branding, following the community imaging guidelines. Two entry sign examples are shown here.

Entry Signage   41

Global Branding

DRIVE Logo

A strong brand identity will represent a consistent standard of quality, and encourage consumer loyalty. The first step in developing a strong brand is to be consistent in the logo reproduction.

Our 3-color master logo has the greatest visual impact and should be used whenever possible.

The Drive logo must contain the following elements arranged in the approved proportions. **No alterations may be made to the logo other than those approved in this book.**

a. Logo Types
The logo may be used in several ways:

   1. Corporate Identity
      Drive Financial Services

   2. Universal Brand

   3. Corporate Icon

In any situation the logo must follow all of the stated criteria.

These logos are available on the enclosed CD. File names are shown in the logo directory.

a1

a2

a3

DRIVE Printed Materials

As the brand continues to grow, so will the look. But a consistent brand concept will project an image of professionalism and uniformity across the board.

There are a few vital elements that are used to create the Drive look. Other than the colors and fonts (which are discussed in detail earlier in the book) Drive also incorporates a significant amount of white space into their printed materials. Full color images are used to add interest and to enhance the white space.

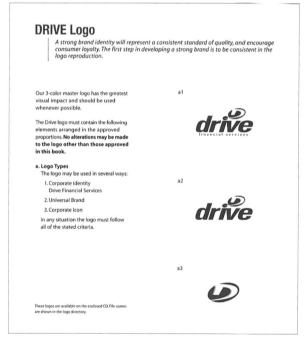

Full Color Images

White Space

Curved Edges

Drive Red

Drive Fonts

Drive Logo

Client
  Drive Financial
Design Firm
  Kendall Creative Shop
Designers
  Jennifer Brehm, Mark K. Platt

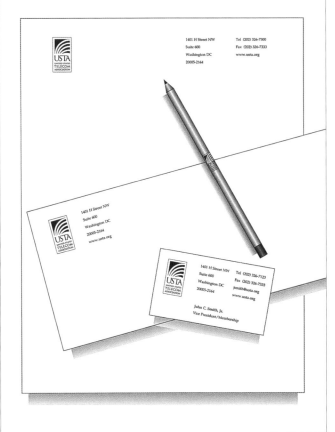

Products　　　　　　Member Identification

23

Products　　　　　　Promotional Items

Front

25

Client
U.S. Telecom Association

Design Firm
Sparkman　+　Associates, Inc.

Designers
Don Sparkman, Melanie Wilkins

Graphic Standards

RIVERMARK

LOGO USE

RIVERMARK

Logo as used in color.

RIVERMARK

Logo as used in a field of color.

RIVERMARK

Logo as used in black and white.

RIVERMARK

Logo as used as a black and white reverse.

Client
Rivermark
Design Firm
Gauger & Silva
Designer
Bob Ankers

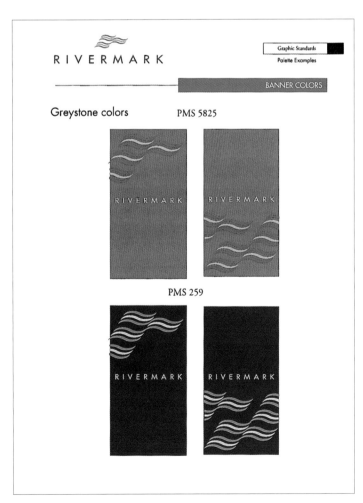

RIVERMARK

Graphic Standards
Palette Examples

BANNER COLORS

Greystone colors   PMS 5825

RIVERMARK

RIVERMARK

PMS 259

RIVERMARK   RIVERMARK

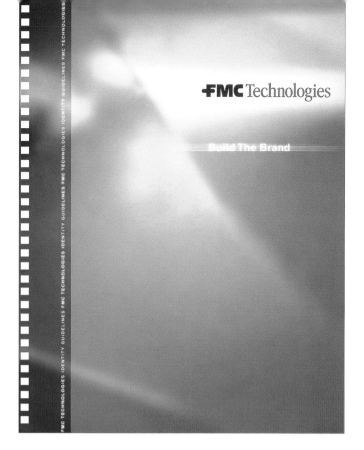

Client
FMC Technologies
Design Firm
Stan Gellman Graphic Design
Designers
Mike Donovan, Barry Tilson

Business Signatures

The signatures below are businesses under the FMC Technologies corporate
name. The guidelines which apply to the FMC Technologies signature also
apply to each of the business signatures.

FMC AirportSystems
FMC EnergySystems
FMC FoodTech

Product Line or Sub-Business Signatures

Approved sub-business unit names may place their names in proximity to the
business signature as follows on marketing materials only, **not on business
cards**, **stationery** or other **correspondence materials**.

FMC AirportSystems
Jetway

FMC EnergySystems
FMC Kongsberg Subsea

FMC FoodTech
Citrus Systems

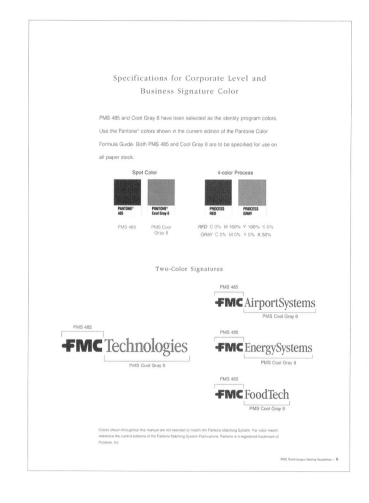

Specifications for Corporate Level and
Business Signature Color

PMS 485 and Cool Gray 8 have been selected as the identity program colors.
Use the Pantone® colors shown in the current edition of the Pantone Color
Formula Guide. Both PMS 485 and Cool Gray 8 are to be specified for use on
all paper stock.

Spot Color   4-color Process

PANTONE®   PANTONE®   PROCESS   PROCESS
485   Cool Gray 8   RED   GRAY

PMS 485   PMS Cool   RED C 0% M 100% Y 100% K 0%
              Gray 8   GRAY C 0% M 0%   Y 0%   K 50%

Two-Color Signatures

PMS 485
FMC AirportSystems
PMS Cool Gray 8

PMS 485
FMC Technologies
PMS Cool Gray 8

PMS 485
FMC EnergySystems
PMS Cool Gray 8

PMS 485
FMC FoodTech
PMS Cool Gray 8

Colors shown throughout this manual are not intended to match the Pantone Matching System. For color match,
reference the current editions of the Pantone Matching System Publications. Pantone is a registered trademark of
Pantone, Inc.

Client
GM

Design Firm
FutureBrand HyperMedia

Designers
Aaron Tobias, Thomas Nguy,
Michael Sheehan, Phil Rufas

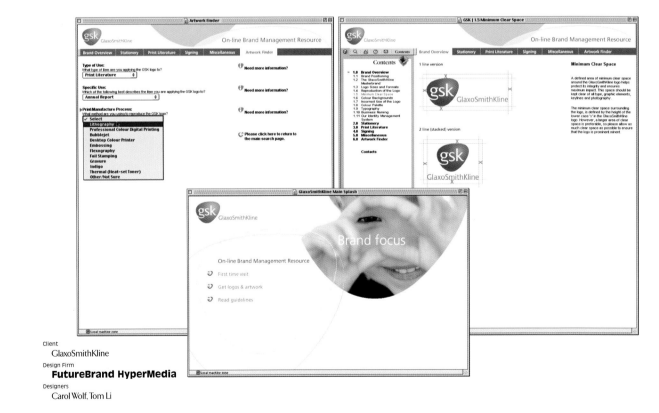

Client
GlaxoSmithKline

Design Firm
FutureBrand HyperMedia

Designers
Carol Wolf, Tom Li

SIGNAGE AND ENVIRONMENTAL GRAPHICS

Client
Sony
Design Firm
Funk/Levis & Associates
Designers
Christopher Berner, Lada Korol

Client
Kiku Obata & Company
Design Firm
Kiku Obata & Company
Designers
Kiku Obata, Kevin Flynn,
Denise Fuehne, Dennis Hyland,
Laura McCanna, Jef Ebers,
Rich Nelson, Julia Schuermann,
Carole Jerome, Cliff Doucet

Client
Rave Motion Pictures
Design Firm
dsgn associates
Design Director
C. Cal Young, AIA
Designer
Nancy P. Weeks

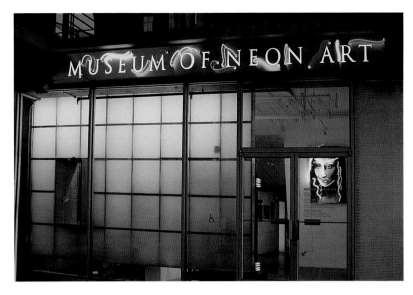

Client
  Museum of Neon Art
Design Firm
  Lili Lakich Studio
Designer
  Lili Lakich

Client
  AIDS Healthcare Foundation
Design Firm
  Lili Lakich Studio
Designer
  Lili Lakich

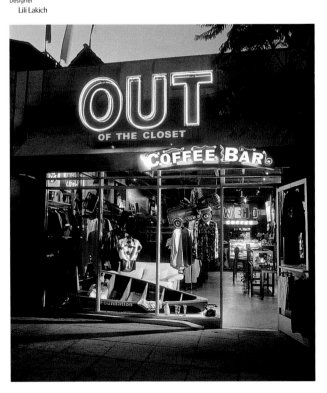

Client
  MBHB—
  McDonnell Boehnen Hulbert & Berghoff
Design Firm
  Studio Blue
Project Manager
  Matthew Simpson
Designers
  Cheryl Towler Weese,
  Kathy Fredrickson,
  Gail Wiener,
  Susan Walsh

Client
King's Seafood Company
Design Firm
30sixty Design, Inc.
Art Director
David Fucellaro
Designer
Duy Nguyen

Client
Torrefazione Italia
Design Firm
Phinney Bischoff Design House
Designers
Dean Hart, Leslie Phinney

Client
General Mills, Inc.
Design Firm
Shea
Designer
Eric Fetrow

Client
Backyard Burgers
Design Firm
King Casey
Designers
John Chrzanowski,
Steve Brent

Client
Kemper Development Company
Design Firm
Michael Courtney Design
Designers
Mike Courtney,
Jennifer Krohn,
Lori Fulsaas

Client
Steiner & Associates
Design Firm
Development Design Group
Designer
Kevin Kern

Client
The Mills Corporation
Design Firm
ID8/RTKL Assoc. Inc.
Designers
Charlie Greenawalt,
Molly Miller, Greg Rose,
Jennifer Cardinal

Client
Phillips Edison
Design Firm
Lorenc + Yoo Design
Designers
Jan Lorenc, Sakchai Rangsiyakorn,
Steve McCall, Susie Caldwell

Client
Port of Seattle/
SeaTac International Airport
Design Firm
NBBJ Graphic Design
Designers
Billy Chen, Eric LeVine

Client
Steiner & Associates
Design Firm
Development Design Group, Inc.
Designer
Curtiss Taylor

Client
Subway
Design Firm
King Casey
Designers
John Chrzanowski,
Steve Brent,
Carolina Guimarey

Client
Kenwood
Design Firm
Jensen Design Associates
Designer
David Jensen

Client
Foth & Van Dyke
Design Firm
Foth & Van Dyke
Designer
Daniel Green
Photography
Studio Forty Four

Client
Storage Way
Design Firm
Bruce Yelaska Design
Designer
Bruce Yelaska

Client
Palladium
Design Firm
Lorenc + Yoo Design
Designers
Jan Lorenc, Steve McCall,
Sakchai Rangsiyakorn

Client
Space Needle
Design Firm
Hornall Anderson Design Works
Designers
Jack Anderson, Cliff Chung,
Mary Hermes, Gretchen Cook,
Andrew Smith, Alan Florsheim

Client
SupplyPro
Design Firm
Laura Coe Design Assoc.
Designer
Tracy Castle

Client
Experience Music Project
Design Firm
NBBJ Graphic Design
Project Manager
Kelly Coller
Designers
Billy Chen, Eric Levine

Client
Hy-Ko Products Company
Design Firm
Kovacs Design
Designer
Carol Kovacs

Client
Sony Computer Entertainment
Design Firm
Creative Dynamics
Designers
Eddie Roberts,
Víctor Rodriguez

Client
  Novell, Inc.
Design Firm
  Hornall Anderson Design Works
Designers
  Larry Anderson, Jack Anderson,
  Cliff Chung, Holly Craven,
  Michael Brugman

Client
  Steiner & Associates
Design Firm
  Development Design Group
Designer
  Kevin Kern

Client
  Cherry Creek Shopping Center
Design Firm
  Ellen Bruss Design
Designers
  Ellen Bruss, G. Carr

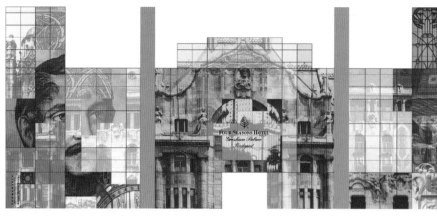

Client
Gresham Palace
Design Firm
Nassar Design
Designers
Nelida Nassar, Margarita Encomienda

Client
Universidad Del Sagrado Corazon
Design Firm
ID Group, Inc.
Designers
Abner Gutierrez, Mayra Maldonado

Client
Schilling Farms
Design Firm
Lorenc + Yoo Design
Designers
Jan Lorenc, David Park,
Steve McCall, Gary Flesher

Client
Cherry Creek
Shopping Center
Design Firm
**Ellen Bruss
Design**
Designer
Ellen Bruss

CORPORATE IMAGE BROCHURES

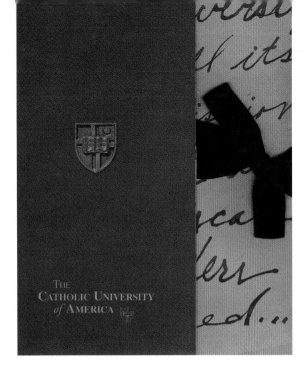

Client
The Catholic University of America
Design Firm
A to Z communications, inc.
Designer
Aimee Lazer

Client
ASU College of Business
Design Firm
Tieken Design & Creative Services
Designer
Fred E. Tieken, Stan Hattaway

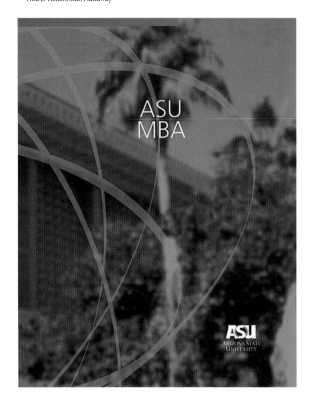

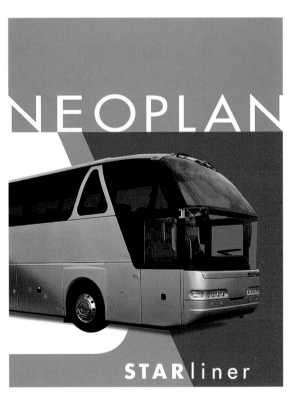

Client
Neoplan USA Corporation
Design Firm
Noble Erickson Inc
Designer
Steven Erickson, Sarah G. Robinson

Client
kor group
Design Firm
kor group
Designer
Anne Callahan, Karen Dendy, M.B. Jaroski
Photographer
Anton Girassl

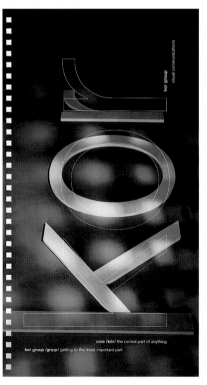

Client
Insignia/ESG
Design Firm
Paradowski Graphic Design
Designer
Steve Cox

Client
Gillespie
Design Firm
Gillespie Design Team
Designers
Jane Keller, George Barrett, Janine
Lazur, Julie Bernardini

Client
LSA Associates, Inc.
Design Firm
Alterpop
Designer
Kimberly Powell

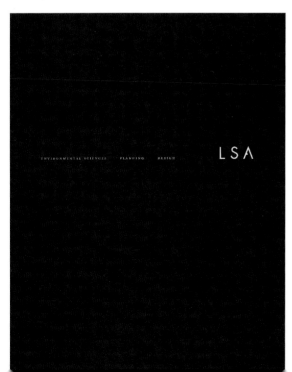

Client
Bruce Bren Homes
Design Firm
Tilka Design
Designer
Sarah Steil

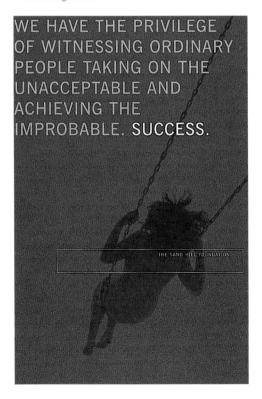

Client
  Fine Arts Museum
Design Firm
  Cahan & Associates
Creative Director
  Bill Cahan
Designer
  Michael Braley

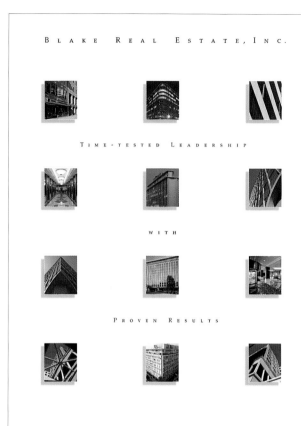

Client
  Blake Real Estate
Design Firm
  Sparkman + Associates, Inc.
Designer
  Don Sparkman

Client
  Starwood
Design Firm
  Gauger & Silva
Designer
  Bob Ankers

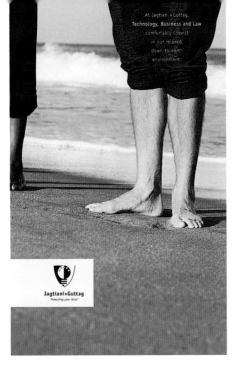

Client
Jagtiani + Guttag
Design Firm
Grasp Creative
Designer
Doug Fuller

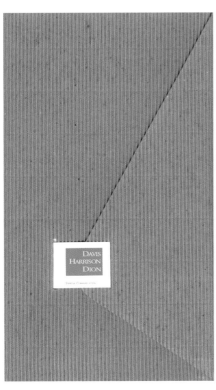

Client
Davis Harrison Dion
Design Firm
Davis Harrison Dion
Designers
Bob Dion, Jennifer Medema

Client
Barra
Design Firm
Addison
Designer
Lindon Leader

Client
General Mills
Design Firm
Liz J. Design, Inc.
Designer
Nancy Hauck

Client
   30sixty Design, Inc.
Design Firm
   30sixty Design, inc.
Art Director
   Par Larsson
Designers
   Craig Peterson, Connie Walters

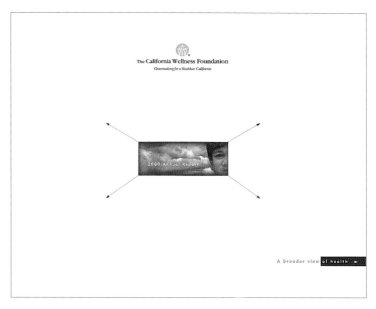

Client
   The California Wellness Foundation
Design Firm
   Hershey Associates
Designers
   Lisa Joss, Richard Vasquez

Client
   Krueger Wright
Design Firm
   Krueger Wright
Designers
   Patrick Kendall, Karen Wright, Joe Morris

Client
   Promistar Financial
Design Firm
   Adam, Filippo & Associates
Designer
   Robert Adam

Client
  Boeing Realty Corporation
Design Firm
  Phinney Bishoff Design House
Designers
  Karin Harris, Dean Hart

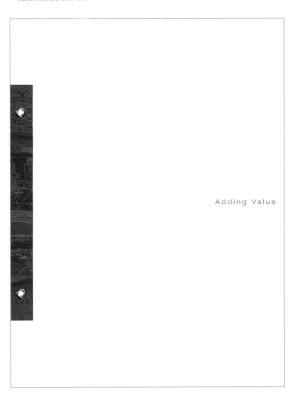

Adding Value

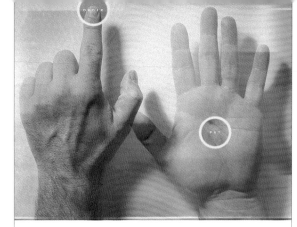

GLOBALCOMMERCE MAKES THE CONNECTION AND STREAMLINES THE FINANCIAL SUPPLY CHAIN FROM ORDER TO PAY.

GLOBALCOMMERCE.
Intelligent Solutions for the Financial Supply Chain

Client
  Global Commerce
Design Firm
  Leopard
Creative Director
  Patrick Cullie
Art Director
  Todd Doyle
Copywriter
  Patrick Cullie

Client
  The Catholic University of America
Design Firm
  A to Z communications, inc.
Designer
  Alan Boarts

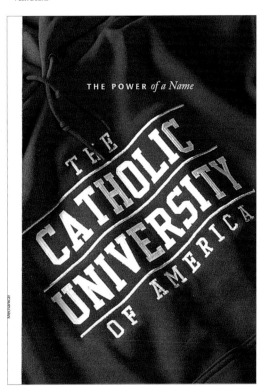

THE POWER *of a Name*

THE
CATHOLIC
UNIVERSITY
OF AMERICA

A great university,

The Campaign for George Mason University

Client
  George Mason University
Design Firm
  Grafik
Designers
  Jonathan Amer, David Collins, Lynn
  Umemoto, Judy Kirpich

Client
Billingsley Company
Design Firm
Kendall Creative Shop
Designers
Tim Childress, Mark K. Platt

Client
Cornell Forge Company
Design Firm
Emphasis Seven Communications, Inc.
Designer
Debra Nemeth

The **New York Academy** *of* **Medicine**

A USER'S GUIDE

Client
NY Academy of Medicine
Design Firm
Lieber Brewster Design, Inc.
Designer
Elisa Carson

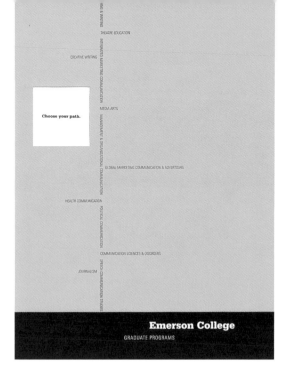

Emerson College
GRADUATE PROGRAMS

Client
Emerson College
Design Firm
kor group
Art Director
Anne Callahan
Designer
James Gibson
Photographers
Jorg Meyer, Tom Katz

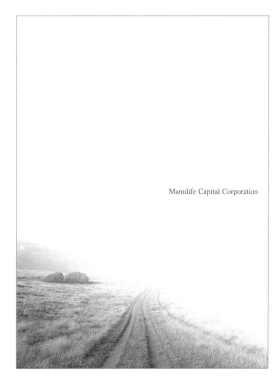

Manulife Capital Corporation

Client
Manulife Capital Corporation
Design Firm
kor group
Art Director
M.B. Jarosik
Designer
James Grady

Client
Converge
Design Firm
kor group
Art Director
M.B. Jarosik
Designers
James Grady, Karen Dendy

CONVERGE

Client
Florsheim Homes
Design Firm
Coakley Heagerty
Designer
Robert Meyerson

Life happens.
Make the most of it in one of our homes.

Client
  Motorola Life Sciences
Design Firm
  Erbe Design
Designers
  Maureen Erbe, Rita Sowins,
  Karen Nakatani

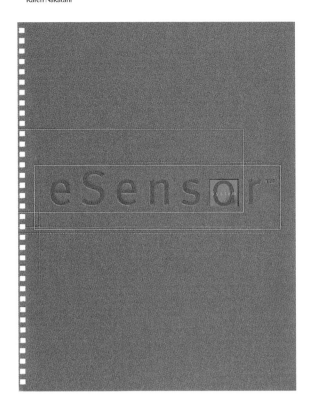

Client
  ComVentures
Design Firm
  Gee + Chung Design
Designers
  Earl Gee, Fani Chung, Kay Wu
Photographer
  Henrik Kam

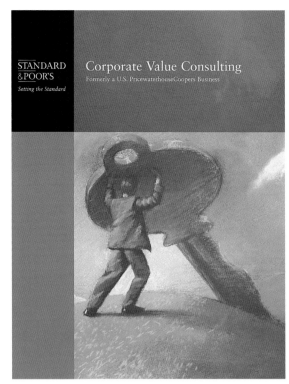

Client
  Standard & Poor's
  Corporate Value Consulting Div.
Design Firm
  Cullinane Design
Designer
  Carmen Li

Client
  Caterpillar Investment Management Ltd.
Design Firm
  **Caterpillar In-house/
  Marketing Communications**
Art Director
  Kenny Beaupre
Designer
  Jennifer Hammontree-Jones
Copywriter
  Samuel Joslin

Client
Klein Bicycle Corporation
Design Firm
Liska + Associates, Inc.
Designer
Brian Graziano, Kim Fry

Client
(i) Structure
Design Firm
Spark Design
Designers
Vince Adam, Joe Gunsten, Rik Boberg

Client
Missouri Botanical Garden
Design Firm
Paradowski Graphic Design
Designer
Steve Cox, Dennis Bland

The Unseen Garden

TO PRESERVE AND ENRICH

Missouri
Botanical
Garden
See the World

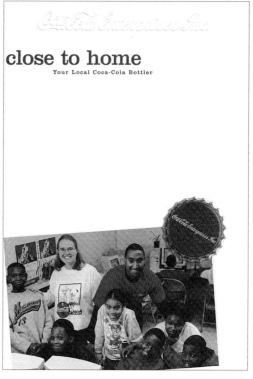

close to home
Your Local Coca-Cola Bottler

Client
Coca-Cola Enterprises, Inc.
Design Firm
Jones Worley Design, Inc.
Designer
Michael Sater

Client
Trammell Crow Residential
Design Firm
Ilium Associates, Inc.
Art Director
Mark Smith
Designer
Angela Hopkins

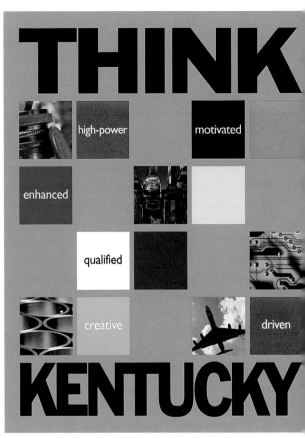

Client
Kentucky Cabinet
for Economic Development
Design Firm
**Rosetta Advertising
& Public Relations**
Designers
Melissa Gausmann, Bill White,
Andrew Sears

Client
DemandTec
Design Firm
1185 Design
Designer
Peggy Burke, Mehdi Anvarian,
Shannon Favata

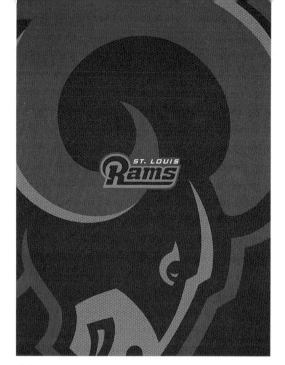

Client
St. Louis Rams
Design Firm
Rodgers Townsend
Designer
Luke Partridge

Client
Navitas Energy
Design Firm
Peggy Lauritsen Design Group
Designer
Michelle Ducayet

Client
The Futures Group International
Design Firm
Dever Designs
Designer
Jeffrey Dever

Client
Sirach Capital Management
Design Firm
Phinney Bischoff Design House
Designers
Dean Hart, Leslie Phinney

Client
  Wirestone
Design Firm
  Dula Image Group
Designer
  Michael Dula

Client
  Sperry
Design Firm
  Phillips Design Group
Designer
  Susan Logcher

Client
  Isogon Corporation
Design Firm
  Communication Graf-fix
Designers
  Ed Sobel, Richard Humann

Client
  Target Corporation
Design Firm
  Target Advertising
Designer
  Dan Weston

Client
  Target Corporation
Design Firm
  Target Advertising
Designer
  Dan Weston

Client
  Box USA
Design Firm
  Connelly Design, Inc.
Creative Director
  Susan Graim
Designer
  Kate Brankin

Client
  Make A Better Place (MABP)
Design Firm
  Liska + Associates, Inc.
Designer
  Paul Wong

Client
  CJ Fox
Design Firm
  Phillips Design Group
Designer
  Susan Logcher

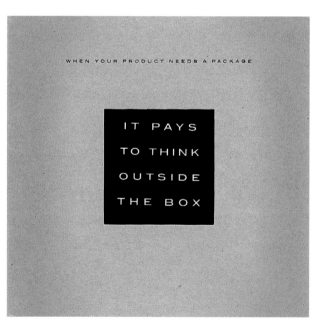

Client
  Omni Media USA
Design Firm
  Karen Skunta & Company
Creative Director
  Karen A. Skunta
Designers
  Christopher Suster,
  Christopher Oldham

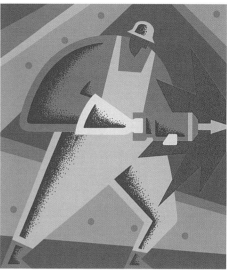

Client
  Center for Nonprofit Management
Design Firm
  Prejean LoBue
Designers
  Gary LoBue, Jr., Kevin Prejean

Client
  NFL Players Inc.
Design Firm
  Grafik
Designers
  Garth Supeville, David Collins

Client
Offset Atlanta
Design Firm
WorldSTAR Design
Designer
Greg Guhl

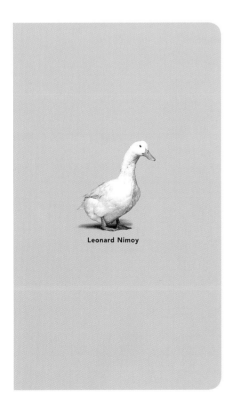

Client
IP revolution
Design Firm
Sacco Group
Designers
Joe Sacco, Kacy Meredith

Client
TIAA-CREF Trust Company
Design Firm
Kiku Obata & Company
Designer
Paul Scherfling

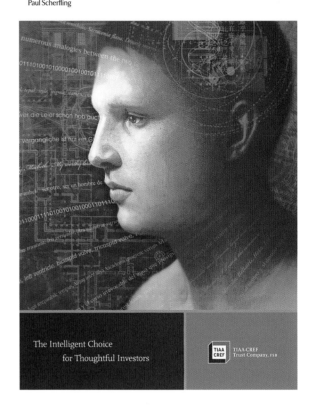

Client
Pacific Symphony Orchestra
Design Firm
Hayden Design
Designer
Tricia Hayden

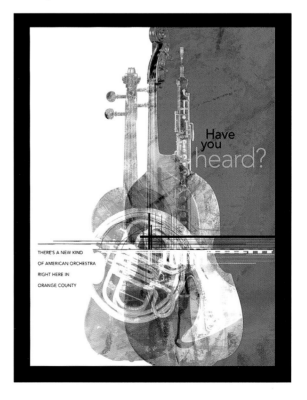

Client
   Chesterfield Day School
Design Firm
   Paradowski Graphic Design
Designers
   Tyson Foersterling, Shawn Cornell

Client
   Thayer Capital
Design Firm
   Sightline Marketing
Designer
   Robert McVearry

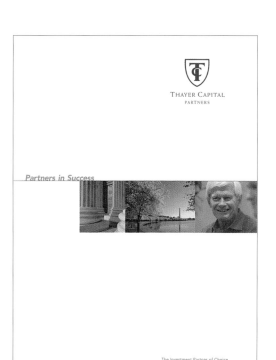

Client
   Photon Dynamics
Design Firm
   1185 Design
Designers
   Peggy Burke, Merry Biggerstaff

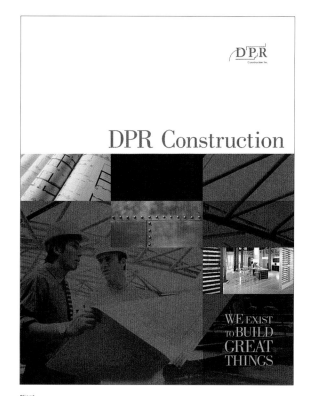

Client
   DPR Construction
Design Firm
   Casper Design Group
Designers
   Kurt Ludwig, Steve Canine

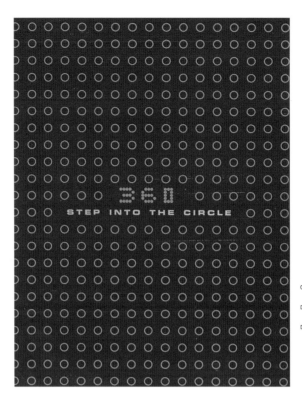

Client
  Target Corporation
Design Firm
  Graphic Culture
Designer
  Cheryl Watson

Client
  Graves Fowler Associates
Design Firm
  Graves Fowler Associates
Designer
  Victoria Q. Robinson

Client
  Drive Financial
Design Firm
  Kendall Creative Shop
Designer
  Jennifer Brehm, Tim Childress,
  Mark K. Platt

WHEN YOU NEED
THE BEST CONTAINERBOARD

當您需要最好的箱板纸時

▲ Weyerhaeuser
The future is growing

Client
 Weyerhaeuser
Design Firm
 Belyea
Art Director
 Patricia Belyea
Designer
 Ron Lars Hansen

Adventure Cruises	14
Glacier Bay Lodge	28
Gates of the Arctic	31
Denali Backcountry	32

ALASKA 🐋 Glacier Bay
CRUISELINE

SMALL SHIP CRUISES AND ADVENTURE TOURS 2002

Client
 Glacier Bay Cruiseline
Design Firm
 Belyea
Art Director
 Patricia Belyea
Designers
 Ron Lars Hansen, Naomi Murphy,
 Anne Dougherty, Kelli Lewis

A New Era In Service
Is Now Here For You.

DOCUMENT
IMAGING Kodak

Client
 Eastman Kodak Company
Design Firm
 Forward branding & identity

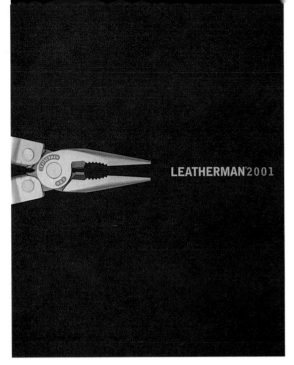

Client
Leatherman Tool Group
Design Firm
**Hornall Anderson
Design Works**
Designers
Jack Anderson, Lisa Cerveny,
Andrew Smith, Andrew Wicklund,
Don Stayner

Client
Doublebridge Technologies
Design Firm
Richland Design Associates
Designers
Judith Richland, Cynthia Zoppa

Client
Avery Dennison
Design Firm
Jensen Design Associates
Art Director
Alyssa Igawa

Client
People Soft
Design Firm
Casper Design Group
Designer
Paul Mussa

Client
Corporate Council for the Arts
Design Firm
NBBJ Graphic Design
Designers
Yachun Peng, Leo Raymundo,
Kelly Coller

Client
Le Saint Géran-Mauritius
Design Firm
**David Carter
Design Associates**
Designer
Gary LoBue, Jr.

Client
Little Dix Bay
Design Firm
**David Carter
Design Associates**
Designer
Ashley Barron Mattocks

Client
    Greater Yield, Ltd.
Design Firm
JA Design Solutions
Designer
    Jean Ashenfelter

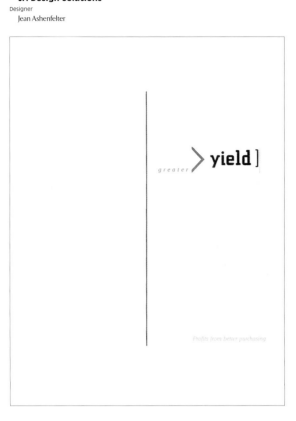

Voice: AIGA National Design Conference 2001 · Marriott Wardman Park Hotel · Washington D.C. · September 23–26, 2001

Client
    AIGA
Design Firm
Cahan & Associates
Creative Director
    Bill Cahan
Designers
    Michael Braley, Bob Dinetz,
    Kevin Roberson, Sharrie Brooks,
    Gary Williams

Client
    Zeppelin Development
Design Firm
Noble Erickson Inc.
Designer
    Jackie Noble, Lisa Scheideler

Client
    Pharmasol
Design Firm
Phillips Design Group
Designer
    Alissa McMahon

Client
Charles Slert Associates
Design Firm
Nicholson Design
Designers
Joe C. Nicholson, Charles Slert

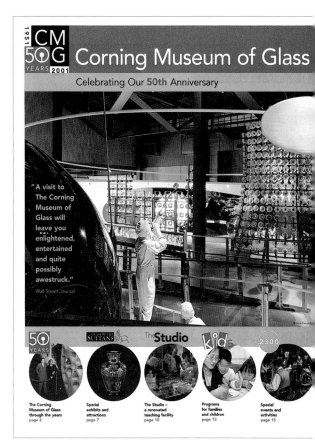

Client
Corning Museum of Glass
Design Firm
Michael Orr + Associates, Inc.
Designers
Michael R. Orr, Thomas Freeland

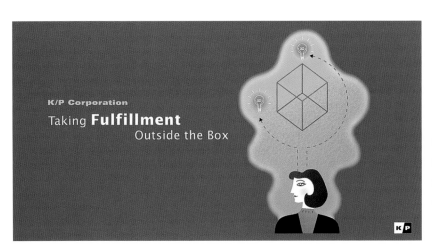

Client
KP Corporation
Design Firm
Belyea
Designer
Anne Dougherty
Illustrator
Bryan Leister

Client
Monaco Coach Corporation
Design Firm
Funk/Levis & Associates
Designer
Alex Wijnen

How will you

ignite

your brand?

Interbrand Hulefeld

Client
Interbrand Hulefeld
Design Firm
Interbrand Hulefeld
Designer
Anita Betz

Client
Allegheny Financial Group
Design Firm
Sewickley Graphics & Design, Inc.
Designer
Michael Seidl

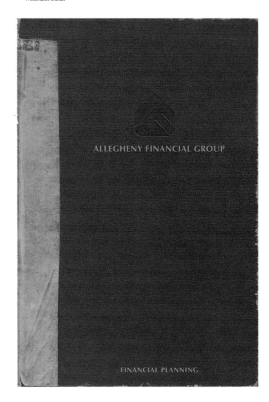

Client
Allegheny Financial Group
Design Firm
Sewickley Graphics & Design, Inc.
Designer
Michael Seidl

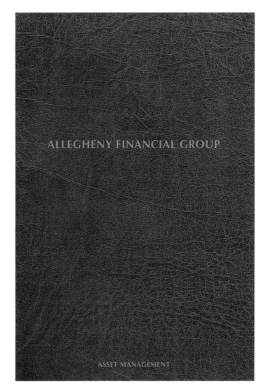

Client
Informa
Design Firm
Richland Design Associates
Designer
Judith Richland, Cynthia Zoppa

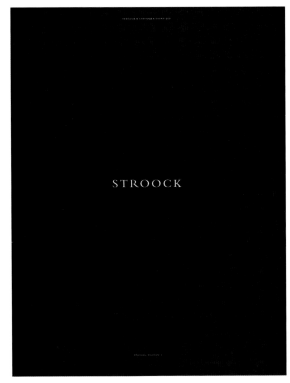

Client
Stroock & Stroock & Lavan
Design Firm
Cahan & Associates
Creative Director
Bill Cahan
Designer
Michael Braley

Client
KCSARC
Design Firm
Belyea
Art Director
Patricia Belyea
Designer
Naomi Murphy
Photographer
Rosanne Olson

Client
U.S. Bancorp Piper Jaffray
Design Firm
Larsen Design + Interactive
Designer
Jo Davison

Client
U.S. Bancorp Piper Jaffray
Design Firm
Larsen Design + Interactive
Designer
Bill Pflipsen

Client
Promistar Financial
Design Firm
Adam, Filippo & Associates
Designers
Larry Geiger, Martin Perez, Robert Adam

Client
Corning Museum of Glass
Design Firm
Michael Orr + Associates, Inc.
Designers
Michael R. Orr, Thomas Freeland

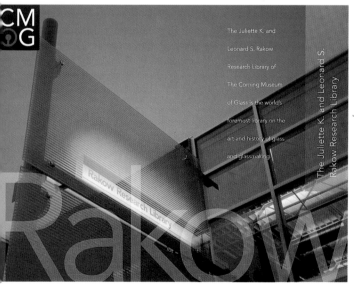

The Juliette K. and Leonard S. Rakow Research Library of The Corning Museum of Glass is the world's foremost library on the art and history of glass and glassmaking.

The Juliette K. and Leonard S. Rakow Research Library

Client
   The College of St. Joseph
Design Firm
   Set?Communicate!
Designer
   Steve Thomas, Dan Wold

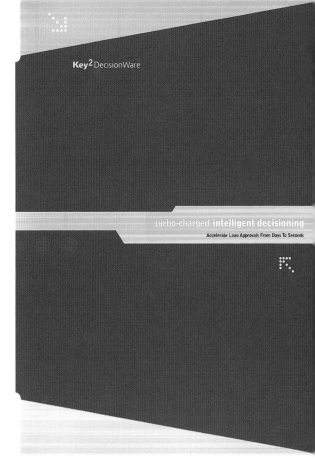

Client
   Keystroke Technology Solutions
Design Firm
   Belyea
Art Director
   Patricia Belyea
Designer
   Ron Lars Hansen

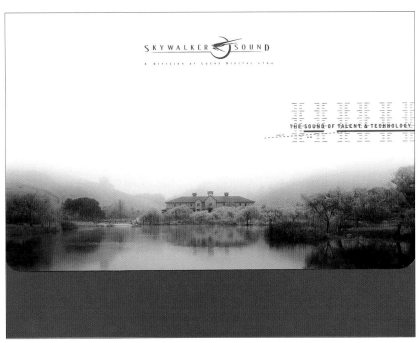

Client
   Skywalker Sound
Design Firm
   Rosenberger Design
Designer
   Shawn Rosenberger

LOGOS

Client
MGM Mirage
Design Firm
Mike Salisbury, L.L.C.
Designer
Leslie Carbaga

Client
Curious Coffee Co.
Design Firm
Merten Design Group
Designer
Tiffany Schmidt

Client
CFW Entertainment
Design Firm
Schum & Associates, Inc.
Designer
Ephraim Schum

Client
Monsanto Company
Design Firm
Stan Gellman Graphic Design
Designers
Jill Lampen, Teresa Thompson

Client
Monsanto Company
Design Firm
Stan Gellman Graphic Design
Designers
Erin Goter,
Teresa Thompson

Client
Tao Tao Chinese Cuisine
Design Firm
Julia Tam Design
Designer
Julia Chong Tam

Client
Sanctuary Bay
Design Firm
Lorenc + Yoo Design
Designers
Jan Lorenc, Susie Caldwell

Client
Strategic Workforce Solutions
Design Firm
Taylor Design
Designers
Hannah Fichandler, Daniel Taylor

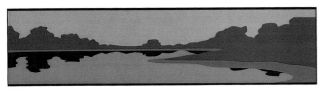

Client
Brighton Avenue Films
Design Firm
Mike Salisbury, L.L.C.
Designers
Daniel Pelaum,
Brian Sieson,
Mike Salisbury

Client
Gateway
Design Firm
Merten Design Group
Designers
Staci Teague,
Terra Gullett-Brown

Client
Coolava
Design Firm
Julia Tam Design
Designer
Julia Chong Tam

Client
Farmclub.com
Design Firm
Arnell Group
Designers
Peter Arnell,
Mike Doyle,
Steven Hankinson

Client
Argonaut
Design Firm
Dan Liew Design
Designers
Dan Liew,
Clive Liew

Client
Joelle Coretti's Team
Design Firm
Rabil & Bates Design
Designer
Seth Sirbaugh

Client
Shea
Design Firm
Shea
Designer
Eric Fetrow

Client
Reebok
Design Firm
Arnell Group
Designers
Peter Arnell,
Jung-Ah Suh,
Jared Richardson

Client
iNetworks
Design Firm
Elias/Savion Advertising
Designers
Ronnie Savion,
Steve Baksis

Client
Rockport
Design Firm
Arnell Group
Designer
Peter Arnell, Jung-Ah Suh

Client
Lawrence & Ponder Ideaworks
Design Firm
Lawrence & Ponder Ideaworks
Designers
Marvie Blair,
Louis Leos,
Gary Fredrickson,
Bil Dicks

Client
Compliance Control, Inc.
Design Firm
Graves Fowler Associates
Designer
Esther J. Kang

Client
Graves Fowler Associates
Design Firm
Graves Fowler Associates
Designer
Victoria Q. Robinson

Client
Mandalay Sports
Design Firm
Hardball Sports
Designers
Michael O'Connell,
John Massé

Client
Jewish Center for Arts + Culture
Design Firm
Gill Fishman Associates
Creative Director
Gill Fishman
Designer
Alicia Ozyjowski

Client
Solar Systems
Design Firm
Heart graphic design
Designer
Clark Most

Client
Reedwood Friends Church
Design Firm
Jeff Fisher LogoMotives
Art Director
Colin Miller
Designer
Jeff Fisher

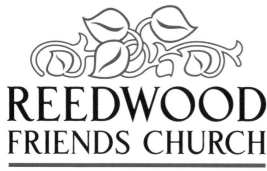

Client
Fun and Food NYC.com
Design Firm
RBG Design, Inc.
Designer
Adam Greiss

Client
Insignia/ESG
Design Firm
Paradowski Graphic Design
Designer
Shawn Cornell

Client
Monsanto
Design Firm
**Paradowski
Graphic Design**
Designer
Steve Cox

Client
Beanstalk
Design Firm
Mindpower, Inc.
Designer
Debi Quilla

Client
New England Firewood Company
Design Firm
Jeff Fisher LogoMotives
Designer
Jeff Fisher

Client
Eastman Kodak Company
Design Firm
Forward branding & identity

Client
Expand Beyond
Design Firm
Liska + Associates, Inc.
Designers
Steve Liska,
Paul Wong

Client
Sherman College of Straight Chiropractic
Design Firm
Set?Communicate!
Designers
Steve Thomas, Dan Wold

Client
California Bento
Design Firm
Crouch and Naegeli/Design Group West
Designer
Jim Naegeli

SHERMAN
COLLEGE
of STRAIGHT
CHIROPRACTIC

CALIFORNIA
BENTO
QUICK HEALTHY FOOD

Client
Regional Aids Interfaith Network
Design Firm
Prejean LoBue
Designers
Kevin Prejean,
Gary LoBue, Jr

Client
Marlin/ConAgra Foods
Design Firm
Prejean LoBue
Designers
Gary LoBue, Jr,
Kevin Prejean

Client
Loftworks
Design Firm
Kiku Obata & Company
Designers
Troy Guzman, Amber Elli

Client
Fundraiser for Twin Towers Relief Fund
Design Firm
Robert Padovano Design
Designers
Robert Padovano,
Ric Ornellas

Client
CFDA
(Council of Fashion Designers of America)
Design Firm
Arnell Group
Designers
Peter Arnell, Mike Doyle

Client
Church of the Beloved
Design Firm
Set?Communicate!
Designers
Steve Thomas, Dan Wold

Client
Eastman Kodak Company
Design Firm
Forward branding & identity

Client
Swain Entertainment
Design Firm
D4 Creative Group
Designer
Andrew Snyder

Gifts & Collectibles

HUTTER Design

TEXAS YOGA

CONVENTION 2001

photography

Client
Bristol-Myers Squibb Company
Design Firm
Health Science Communications, Inc.
Designer
Robert Padovano

Client
Genentech Bio Oncology
Design Firm
Health Science Communications, Inc.
Designer
Robert Padovano

2002 DIABETES
EDUCATION FACULTY
CONFERENCE

THE VISITING FACULTY PROGRAM ON
METASTATIC BREAST CANCER

Client
Vino.com
Design Firm
Berkeley Design L.L.C.
Designer
Larry Torno

Client
Saints Leo-Seton School
Design Firm
Prejean LoBue
Designers
Kevin Prejean,
Gary LoBue, Jr.

Client
International Association of Amusement Parks and Attractions
Design Firm
Kircher
Designer
Bruce E. Morgan

Client
National Postal Forum
Design Firm
McGaughy Design
Designer
Malcolm McGaughy

FALL 2001
DENVER
COLORADO
OCTOBER 14-17

Client
First Baptist Church Woodstock
Design Firm
Lorenc + Yoo Design
Designers
Chung Youl Yoo, David Park

Client
Mike Salisbury
Design Firm
Mike Salisbury, L.L.C.
Designer
Robert Grossman

Client
Alien Technology Corporation
Design Firm
Cymbic
Creative Director
Kenichi Nishiwaki
Designer
Scott Jackson

Client
State Colleges of Massachusetts
Design Firm
DavisPartners
Creative Director
Tom Davis
Designer
Ken Cool

Client
Cymbic
Design Firm
Cymbic
Creative Director
Kenichi Nishiwaki
Designers
Amanda Ely,
Joanna Dolby,
Michael Fu-Ming

Client
Beverly Hills Dentistry
Design Firm
Strata Media
Art Directors, Designers
Richard Vasquez, Chris Conant

Client
John Templeton Foundation
Design Firm
D4 Creative Group
Designer
Wicky Lee

THE INSTITUTE FOR RESEARCH ON
UNLIMITED LOVE

Client
The Stephen Decatur House Museum
Design Firm
**Schum &
Associates, Inc.**
Designers
Guy-Franz Schum,
Randall Pope

The STEPHEN
DECATUR
HOUSE
MUSEUM
His House. Our History.

Client
OPUS
Design Firm
Shea
Designer
Jason Wittwer

Client
Henderson Architectural Group
Design Firm
Parola Design Assoc.
Designer
Michael Parola

Henderson | Architectural Group, Inc.

Client
Nutiva
Design Firm
Cymbic
Creative Director
Kenichi Nishiwaki
Designer
Michael Fu-Ming

Nutiva
NOURISHING PEOPLE & PLANET
TM

Client
24 by 7 Dating
Design Firm
PM Design
Designers
Philip Maizzo,
Andrei Koribanics

24 by 7
DATING

Client
Microsoft X Box
Design Firm
B.D. Fox & Friends, Inc.
Designer
Damon Thompson

Client
Topaz Partners
Design Firm
Gill Fishman Associates
Creative Director
Gill Fishman
Designer
Tammy Torrey

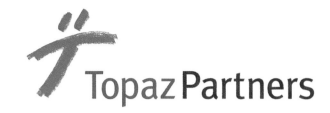

Client
Montana Eyes
Design Firm
Mike Salisbury, L.L.C.
Designer
Nina Weisbeck

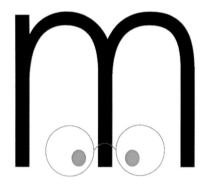

Client
Babalu
Design Firm
PM Design
Designers
Philip Maizzo, Andrei Koribanics

*Neuvo Latino
Restaurant & Night Club*

Client
Merten Design Group
Design Firm
Merten Design Group
Designer
Barry Merten

MERTEN

DESIGN

GROUP

Client
Con Edison
Design Firm
Arnell Group
Designers
Peter Arnell, Mike Doyle

Client
St. Coletta & Cardinal Cushing
Design Firm
Hill Holliday
Designers
Melissa O'Faherty, Mina Kalemkeryan

St.Coletta & Cardinal Cushing
SCHOOLS OF MASSACHUSETTS

Client
Sierra Nevada College
Design Firm
Mindpower, Inc.
Designers
Niki Walker, Shannon Peterson

Sierra Nevada College
THE LIBERAL ARTS AT LAKE TAHOE

Client
Rails to Trails Conservancy
Design Firm
Stan Gellman Graphic Design
Designers
Erin Goter, Mike Donovan

TRAILLINK
2001
The 3rd International
Trails and Greenways Conference

Client
Silver Spring Presbyterian Church Children's Center
Design Firm
Graves Fowler Associates
Designers
Jim Nuttle, Kristin Braaten
Illustrator
Jim Nuttle

SSPC Children's Center

Client
Nyhus Communications
Design Firm
Hansen Design Company
Designers
Pat Hansen, Jacqueline Smith

Client
Applied Wave Research, Inc.
Design Firm
Poonja Design
Designer
Suleman Poonja

Client
Whittier Wood Products
Design Firm
Poppie Advertising Design, Inc.
Designer
James Hershiser

Client
Christ's Church
Design Firm
Belyea
Designer
Ron Lars Hansen

Client
Brookfield Properties
Design Firm
Shea
Designers
Eric Fetrow, James Rahn

Client
Union College
Design Firm
Mindpower, Inc.
Designer
Tony Thomas

Client
Vue Lodge
Design Firm
Belyea
Art Director
Patricia Belyea
Designer
Ron Lars Hansen

Client
Cyntric
Design Firm
Cymbic
Creative Director
Kenichi Nishiwaki
Designers
Amanda Ely,
Ken Kubo, Yong An

Client
Zaidee Coco
Design Firm
Eddins Madison Creative
Creative Director
Marcia Eddins
Art Director
Jeff Roberts

Client
ComVentures
Design Firm
Gee + Chung Design
Designer
Earl Gee, Fani Chung

Client
Glacier Bay Cruiseline
Design Firm
Belyea
Art Director
Patricia Belyea
Designers
Ron Lars Hansen, Naomi Murphy

Client
LSI Logic
Design Firm
Parola Design
Designer
Michael Parola

Client
Merv Griffin Hotels
Design Firm
Mike Salisbury, L.L.C.
Designer
Leslie Carbaga

Client
Visual Arts
Design Firm
Flourish
Designers
Christopher Ferranti, Henry Frey, Jing Lauengco

Client
Microsoft XBox
Design Firm
B.D. Fox & Friends
Designer
Brett Wooldridge
Letterforms
Mike Salisbury

Client
Running with Scissors
Design Firm
Richard Zeid Design
Designer
Richard Zeid
Illustrator
Ann Boyd

Client
Uptown Community Action Group
Design Firm
Adam, Filippo & Associates
Designers
Adam, Filippo & Associates

Client
design 9ll/Quinlan DesignWorks
Design Firm
Quinlan DesignWorks
Designer
Steven Quinlan

Client
Bruce Riccitelli
Design Firm
PM Design
Designer
Philip Marzo

Client
Panda
Design Firm
Mike Salisbury, L.L.C.
Designers
Mike Salisbury, Travis Page

Client
JulieJulie
Design Firm
Stahl Design Inc
Designer
David Stahl

Client
Orange County Museum & Art
Design Firm
Mike Salisbury, L.L.C.
Designers
Mike Salisbury, Bob Maile,
Maryevelyn McGough

Client
Bi-Fi Records
Design Firm
Matt Travaille Graphic Design
Designer
Matt Travaille

Client
Colorado Bar Assoc.
Design Firm
Rassman Design
Designers
John Rassman, Glen Hobbs

Client
Red Canoe
Design Firm
Red Canoe
Art Director
Deb Koch
Designer
Caroline Kavanagh

Client
Clear Blue Sky Productions
Design Firm
Methodologie
Designer
Gabe Goldman

Client
SILK–New York
(world-class cabaret)
Design Firm
JDC Design, Inc.
Designer
Valentina Kogan

Client
Wet Dawg
Design Firm
Funk/Levis & Associates
Designer
Beverly Soasey

Client
Upper Deck Company
Design Firm
Glitschka Studios
Designer
Von R. Glitschka

Client
Hawaiian Airlines
Design Firm
Addison
Designers
David Schuemann, Lindon Leader

Client
Aunt Irene's Care Packages
Design Firm
Octavo Designs
Designers
Sue Hough, Eryn Althouse

Client
The John F. Kennedy, Jr. Institute for
Worker Education/Reaching Up
Design Firm
Jasper Design
Designers
Lysa Opfer, Jim Jasper

Client
GVG Aesthetics–
Eyelid & Facial Enhancement
Design Firm
Insight Design Communications
Designers
Marc Bosworth,
Tracy Holdeman

Client
Marin Community Foundation
Design Firm
Driscoll Design
Designer
Terri Driscoll

MARIN COMMUNITY FOUNDATION

Client
Food Bank of Corpus Christi
Design Firm
Morehead, Dotts & Associates
Designers
Roy Smith, Jim Forsythe

F O O D
B A N K
C O R P U S
C H R I S T I

Client
Carlos O'Kelly's–Hog Wild
Design Firm
Insight Design Communications
Designers
Sherrie and Tracy Holdeman

Client
Crystal Farms
Design Firm
Compass Design
Designers
Bill Collins, Tom Arthur, Rich McGowen

Client
Ketchum for Heinz
Design Firm
A to Z communications, inc.
Designer
Chris Konopack

Client
Long John Silver's
Design Firm
Design Forum
Creative Director
Bill Chidley

Client
Peer-Vue LLC
Design Firm
Grasp Creative
Designers
Aaron Taylor, Doug Fuller

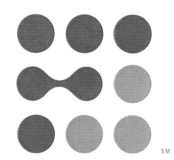

Client
Brahmacom
Design Firm
ilumina
Designers
Kevin Bergen, Todd Kinniburgh,
Annalli Skaar, Kevin O'Leary

Client
Fuszion Collaborative
Design Firm
Fuszion Collaborative
Designer
Tony Fletcher

Client
Force 10 Motor Sports
Design Firm
Planit
Designer
Molly Stevenson

Client
The Body Positive
Design Firm
Landor Associates
Design Director
Dean Wilcox
Designer
Ayo Seligman

Client
Who's Calling.com
Design Firm
Hansen Design Company
Designers
Pat Hansen, Jacqueline Smith

Client
MoMA—Museum of Modern Art
Design Firm
Deka Design
Designer
Dmitry Krasny

Client
Dr. B. Mark Hammonds
Design Firm
**Renaissance
Media Conepts**
Designer
Bo Parker

Client
Bristol-Myers Squibb
Design Firm
Fire House Inc.
Designer
Bob Young

Client
Mandalay Sports
Design Firm
Hardball Sports
Designers
Michael O'Connell, John Massé

Client
Optelec
Design Firm
Millyard Design Assoc. Ltd.
Designers
H.B. Millyard, Abigail Scholz

Client
The Golf Digest Companies
Design Firm
McMillian Design
Designer
William McMillian

Client
Laura's House Transitional Center
Design Firm
Bradfield Design/Max Marketing
Designer
Debra Bradfield

OCEAN CITY
AMATEUR CLASSIC

LAURA'S HOUSE
STEP AHEAD LIVING CENTER

Client
Silver Bullet Strategies
Design Firm
McGaughy Design
Designer
Malcolm McGaughy

Client
William Penn Foundation
Design Firm
Art 270, Inc.
Designers
John Opet, Carl Mill

WILLIAM PENN
FOUNDATION

Client
Kelly Ripken
Design Firm
Planit
Designer
Kelli Thrasher

Client
Transhield
Design Firm
Planit
Designer
John Klemstein

TRANSHIELD

Client
Pardee Homes
Design Firm
Greenhaus
Designers
Tracy Sabin, Craig Fuller,
Sandra Sharp

CANYON
HILLS

Client
Simpson Housing Limited Partnership
Design Firm
Noble Erickson Inc
Designers
Robin H. Ridley, Steven Erickson

PENTERRA PLAZA

Client
August Schell Brewing Co.
Design Firm
Compass Design
Designers
Tom Arthur,
Mitch Lindgren,
Rich McGowen

Client
Sabingrafik, Inc.
Design Firm
Sabingrafik, Inc.
Designer
Tracy Sabin

Client
Studio Products Inc.
Design Firm
Lee Busch Design
Designers
Lee Busch, Andree Cordella

Client
United Way of America/National Football League
Design Firm
Rottman Creative Group, LLC
Designer
Gary Rottman

Client
BellSouth
Design Firm
HardBall Sports
Designers
Michael O'Connell, Andy Gosendi

Client
Daddy Sam's
Design Firm
Compass Design
Designers
Tom Arthur,
Bill Collins

Client
Virtual Gourmet
Design Firm
Mindpower, Inc.
Designer
Niki Walker

Client
Mark Brooks Golf
Design Firm
Graphic Concepts Group
Designer
Brian Wilburn

Client
Natural Selection Foods
Design Firm
Takigawa Design
Designers
Jerry Takigawa, Jay Galster

Client
Provision X
Design Firm
Edelman Design Worldwide
Designer
Teresa Costantini, Joe Ondrla

Client
Big Behr Design Co.
Design Firm
Big Behr Design Co.
Designers
Tracy Sabin, Randy Behr, Mike Hurstad

Client
Tres Vineyard
Design Firm
The Wecker Group
Designer
Robert Wecker

Client
The James Buchanan Foundation
Design Firm
Dean Design/Marketing Group, Inc.
Designer
Jeff Phillips

Client
Mainstreet
Design Firm
Hunter Advertising
Designer
Carolyn J. Hunter

Client
Chamber of Music Society
Design Firm
Tilka Design
Designers
Sarah Steil, Colleen Brennan

Client
Plymouth Thread
Design Firm
The Design Group
Designer
David Gibbs

Client
Mississippi Valley State University
Design Firm
Set?Communicate!
Designers
Steve Thomas, Dan Wold

Client
Texas A&M University—Corpus Christi
Design Firm
Morehead, Dotts & Associates
Designer
Roy Smith

Design Firm
Anna Ohalla,Inc.

Design Firm
Anna Ohalla, Inc.

Client
greens.com
Design Firm
Sabingrafik, Inc.
Designers
Tracy Sabin, Dann Wilson

Client
Boykin Lodging Company
Design Firm
Epstein Design Partners, Inc.
Designers
Liha Linahan, John Okal

Client
Greensboro Radiology
Design Firm
The Design Group
Designers
Bob Nutt, David Gibbs

Client
Brinker International
Design Firm
Addison Whitney
Designers
Kimberlee Davis, Lisa Johnston, David Houk

GREENSBORO
RADIOLOGY
THE MEDICAL IMAGING PROFESSIONALS

Client
SpringHaven
Design Firm
VIVIDESIGN Group

Client
The Painters Inc.
Design Firm
Gage Design
Designer
Chris Roberts

Client
Acadia Board Co., LTD
Design Firm
G1440, Inc.
Designer
Jason H. Thornton

Client
Volaris Advisors
Design Firm
Frankfurt Balkind
Designer
David Suh

Client
   Vertical Properties Group
Design Firm
   Brand, Ltd
Designers
   Scott Wizell,
   Virginia Thompson Martino

Client
   WealthCycle
Design Firm
   Michael Patrick Partners
Designers
   Jenny Herrick, Brian Hilton

Design Firm
   Monster Design

Client
   Plaza Apartments
Design Firm
   McMillian Design
Designer
   William McMillian

Client
   Allen Miller Golf
Design Firm
   Crowley Webb and Associates
Designer
   Jeff Pappalardo

Client
   Redington LLC
Design Firm
   DavisPartners
Creative Director
   Tom Davis
Designer
   Liz Fedorzyn

Client
Kelleen Griffin
Design Firm
Design-Nut
Designer
Brent M. Almond

Client
First Presbyterian Church of Germantown
Design Firm
Art 270, Inc.
Designer
Nicole Ganz

THE FIRST PRESBYTERIAN

CHURCH IN GERMANTOWN

Client
TOLD Development Company
Design Firm
Peggy Lauritsen Design Group
Designer
Laura Dokken

Client
Lifetime Optometry
Design Firm
Zeal Creative
Designers
Heesyun Ruettgers, Paul Ruettgers

Client
Parkside Community Associates
Design Firm
Crowley Webb and Associates
Designer
Pete Reiling

Client
Vision Management Association
Design Firm
Crowley Webb and Associates
Designer
Kelly Gambino

Past Present Parkside

VMA, LLC

Client
TTI
Design Firm
Graphic Concepts Group
Designer
Brian Wilburn

Client
LiveFiles.com
Design Firm
Zeal Creative
Designer
Paul Ruettgers

Client
Flint Hills Resources
Design Firm
Koch Creative Services
Designer
Brad Ruder

Client
Grandie Foods
Design Firm
Mark Oliver, Inc.
Designers
Mark Oliver, Brenna Pierce, Patty Driskel

Client
White Castle System Inc.
Design Firm
Design forum
Creative Director
Bill Chidley

Client
Zook's Harley Davidson
Design Firm
Sayles Graphic Design
Designer
John Sayles

Client
Oklahoma State University
Design Firm
Semio Design
Art Director, Designer
Justin Johnson

Client
XTO Energy
Design Firm
Graphic Concepts Group
Designer
Brian Wilburn

Client
Myriagon
Design Firm
Kendall Creative Shop
Designers
Jennifer Brehm, Mark K. Platt

Client
New Life Mission Church
Design Firm
Zeal Creative
Designer
Heesyun Ruettgers

Client
Sol Y Luna
Design Firm
tompertdesign
Designers
Claudia Huber Tompert, Michael Tompert

Client
Carhop
Design Firm
Sayles Graphic Design
Designer
John Sayles

Client
Bamboo Asian Bistro & Bar
Design Firm
Funk/Levis & Associates
Designers
Beverly Soasey, David Funk

Client
Dan Steckline
Design Firm
Aufuldish & Warinner
Designer
Kathy Warinner

ACANTHUS
CUSTOM CABINETS

Client
Splash PG, Inc
Design Firm
The Partnership, Inc.
Designer
Sim Wong

Client
Parkway Hills Baptist Church
Design Firm
Briley & Stables Creative
Designer
Dan Stables

deep**H2O**
PARKWAY HILLS YOUTH

Client
Rheologics
Design Firm
Frankfurt Balkind
Designer
David Suh

Client
eBridge
Design Firm
Funk/Levis & Associates
Designers
Christopher Berner, David Funk

RH≡OLOGICS

eBridge

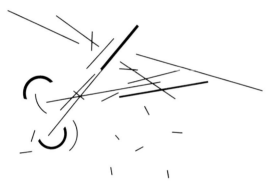

Client
McBee Homes
Design Firm
Graphic Concepts Group
Designer
Brian Wilburn

Client
Adventures in Paradise
Design Firm
Grasp Creative
Designers
Doug Fuller, Aaron Taylor

Client
Arlington Symphony
Design Firm
Grasp Creative
Designers
Doug Fuller,
Aaron Taylor

ARLINGTON
Symphony

Client
Cici's Enterprises
Design Firm
Design Forum
Designers
Bruce Dybvad and Team

Client
High Falls Brewing Company
Design Firm
McElveney & Palozzi Design Group
Designers
Jon Westfall,
Nick Woyciesjes,
Mike Johnson

Client
Maryland Works, Inc.
Design Firm
Dever Designs
Designers
Jeffrey Dever, Chris Komisar

Client
Side H2O productions
Design Firm
**Joel Katz
Design Associates**
Designers
Jennifer Long, Joel Katz

Client
Triangle Montessori
Design Firm
Greg Welsh Design
Designer
Greg Welsh

Client
Thorn Creek Development Corporation
Design Firm
Sewickley Graphics & Design, Inc.
Designer
Michael Seidl

Client
Ford Consulting Group
Design Firm
Tilka Design
Designer
Sarah Steil

Client
Second & Main
Design Firm
Graphica
Designers
Susan Doren Kemper.
Cindy Schnell

Client
AGIA
Design Firm
Mark Oliver, Inc.
Designer
Mark Oliver

Client
Car-X Service Systems Inc.
Design Firm
Design North
Senior Design Director
Mark Topczewski

Client
LogoMotion
Design Firm
Foundation23, Inc.
Designer
Ken Roberts

Client
Bright Rain Creative
Design Firm
Bright Rain Creative
Designers
Kevin Hough, Matt Marino

Client
Digital Online Network
Design Firm
Brandville.com
Designer
Michelle Suazo

Client
Tandoori Nights
Design Firm
Levine & Associates
Designer
Monica Snellings

Client
Tarrant County Republican Party
Design Firm
Renaissance Media Concepts
Designer
Bo Parker

Client
Visteon
Design Firm
Paradowski Graphic Design
Designer
Shawn Cornell

Client
Carol Pyrum Photography
Design Firm
Renaissance Media Concepts
Designer
Bo Parker

Client
Wolfgang Puck/Walters Group
Design Firm
Ripple Strategic Design & Consulting
Designer
Raymond Perez

Client
Frix Jennings Clinic
Design Firm
Levine & Associates
Designer
Dana Craig

Client
Liz Shapiro Legal Search
Design Firm
Randi Wolf Design, Inc.
Designer
Randi Wolf

Client
Coastal Enterprises
Design Firm
Gunion Design
Designer
Jefrey Gunion

Client
Morrow Development
Design Firm
Roni Hicks & Assoc.
Designers
Tracy Sabin, Steve Sharp

Client
Plug-in
Design Firm
Steve Naegele Design
Designer
Steve Naegele

Client
Wine Design
Design Firm
Brand, Ltd
Designer
Virginia Thompson Martino

Client
Barb's Studio 104
Design Firm
ZGraphics, Ltd.
Art Director
LouAnn Zeller
Designer
Kris Martinez Farrell

Client
Gourmet Cellars
Design Firm
Michael Niblett Design
Designer
Michael Niblett

Client
AskCredit.com
Design Firm
Zeal Creative
Designers
Paul Ruettgers, Heesyun Ruettgers

Client
Mosaic Youth Theater
Design Firm
Pangborn Design, Ltd.
Designer
Dominic Pangborn

Client
gN Solutions
Design Firm
Mires
Creative Director
Jose Serrano
Designer
Joy Price

276

Client
American Urological Association
Levine & Associates
Designer
Randi Wright

Client
Pope John Paul II Cultural Center
Grafik Marketing Communications
Designers
Michelle Mar, Judy Kirpich

POPE JOHN PAUL II
▪ CULTURAL CENTER ▪

Client
Clayco Construction Company/Central Insti.
Bright Rain Creative
Designer
Kevin Hough

Client
Lindt and Sprungli
Design Forum
Creative Director
Scott Smith

Client
Abington Art Center
Art 270, Inc.
Designers
Carl Mill, John Opet

ABINGTON
ART CENTER

Client
Ican
Sacco Group
Designer
Jeff Kavan

ICAN

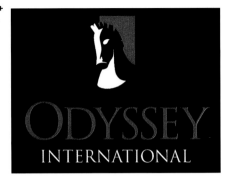

COLORADO
CONSERVATION
TRUST

GoodwillCommunications

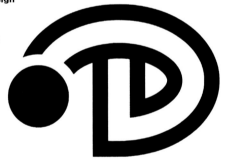

otto's duds & suds

The Wild Animal Clinic
B E N E F I T

Client
Crystal Farms
Design Firm
Compass Design
Designers
Bill Collins, Tom Arthur, Mitch Lindgren

Client
Oakwood Homes
Design Firm
Rassman Design
Designers
Lyn D'Amato, Chandra Sandoval

Client
Cornerstone Customer Solutions
Design Firm
Sacco Group
Designer
Jeff Kavan

Client
urbanfirecompany.com
Design Firm
Mindpower, Inc.
Designer
Niki Walker

Client
David Cohen
Design Firm
Design-Nut
Designer
Brent M. Almond

Client
Java Junction
Design Firm
Rabil & Bates Design
Designer
Seth Sirbaugh

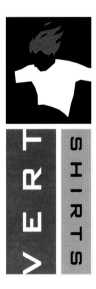

Client
Opryland Hotel—Nashville
Design Firm
Lorenc + Yoo Design
Designers
Jan Lorenc,
Susie Caldwell,
David Park

Client
TC Graham Associates
Design Firm
Mona MacDonald Design
Designer
Mona MacDonald

Client
Make A Better Place (MABP)
Design Firm
Liska + Associates, Inc.
Designer
Fernando Munoz

Client
inOvate
Design Firm
Dula Image Group
Designer
Michael Dula

Client
National Cattlemen's Exchange
Design Firm
DesignWorks Group
Designer
Stephen St. John

Client
Opryland Hotel—Nashville
Design Firm
Lorenc + Yoo Design
Designers
Jan Lorenc,
Susie Caldwell,
David Park

Client
Deleo Clay Tile Company
Design Firm
Mires
Creative Director
José Serrano
Designer, Illustrator
Miguel Perez

Client
Eight Hills Catering
Design Firm
Callery & Company
Designer
Kelley Callery

Client
Central Michigan University
Design Firm
Heart graphic design
Designer
Clark Most

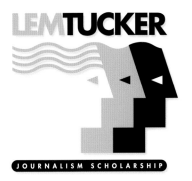

Client
Subway
Design Firm
Tieken Design & Creative Services
Designers
Fred E. Tieken, Lisette Sacks

Client
Banner, Briley & White
Design Firm
DesignWorks Group
Designer
Stephen St. John

Client
Opryland Hotel–Nashville
Design Firm
Lorenc + Yoo Design
Designers
Jan Lorenc,
Susie Caldwell,
David Park

Client
Stan Helfrich
Design Firm
Paradowski Graphic Design
Designer
Shawn Cornell

Client
Summertech
Design Firm
Deka Design
Designer
Dmitry Krasny

Client
Continuum Partners
Design Firm
Ellen Bruss Design
Designers
Ellen Bruss,
Charles Carpenter

Client
Continuum Partners
Design Firm
Ellen Bruss Design
Designers
Ellen Bruss,
Charles Carpenter

Client
Lincoln Properties
Design Firm
Art 270, Inc.
Designer
Nicole Ganz

Client
Silver Bridge
Design Firm
Set?Communicate!
Designers
Steve Thomas, Dan Wold

Client
Brick Red Records
Design Firm
**Tornado
Design**
Designers
Al Quattrocchi,
Jeff Smith

Client
School Communities That Work
Design Firm
Re: Creative
Designers
Tim Eng, Johnny Chau

Client
Power Market
Design Firm
Meta Design
Designers
Carlo Bernouli, Tim Holmes,
Jerry Knight, Rick Lowe

Client
San Luis Obispo Eye Associates
Design Firm
Pierre Rademaker Design
Designers
Pierre Rademaker, Kenny Swete

Client
VOTA & Associates
Design Firm
VAL Designs
Designer
Lan Hoang Vu

Client
People Gotta Eat
Design Firm
Kendall Creative Shop
Designer
Mark K. Platt

Client
Saint Clair Press
Design Firm
Stahl Design Inc
Designer
David Stahl

Client
Teague Freyaldenhoven Freyaldenhoven
Design Firm
The Design Group
Designers
David Gibbs, David Graves

SAINT CLAIR PRESS

TEAGUE
FREYALDENHOVEN
FREYALDENHOVEN
ARCHITECTS & PLANNERS, LLP

Client
St. Paul Chamber Orchestra
Design Firm
Liz J. Design, Inc.
Designer
Bryan Barnes

Client
Enerphaze
Design Firm
Klündt Hosmer Design
Designers
Darin Klündt, Eric Grinstead,
Judy Heggem-Davis

Client
Hi-Res Music
Design Firm
Tornado Design
Designers
Al Quattrocchi,
Jeff Smith

Client
NC A&T State University
Design Firm
Set?Communicate!
Designers
Steve Thomas, Dan Wold

Client
Gloria Dei Lutheran Church
Design Firm
'Tudes
Designer
Sandy Newcomb

Client
Advantage Partners
Design Firm
**Epstein Design
Partners, Inc.**
Designer
Gina Linahan

Client
American Boychoir
Design Firm
Howard Design Group
Designer
Peter Gialloreto

Client
The Sewickley Gallery
Design Firm
Sewickley Graphics & Design, Inc.
Designer
Michael Seidl

Client
Foulsten Siefkin—Attorneys at Law
Design Firm
Insight Design Communications
Designers
Sherrie & Tracy Holdeman

Client
Supringo!
Design Firm
**Axis Design
Communications, Inc.**
Designer
Holly T. Stein

Client
Convenas Solutions
Design Firm
Crowley Webb and Associates
Designer
Ann Casady

Client
Advanced Vision Laser Center
Design Firm
Morehead, Dotts & Associates
Designer
Gilbert Cantu

Client
Swenson Say Fagét
Design Firm
Gage Design
Designer
Chris Roberts

Client
Libretto
Design Firm
Lee Busch Design
Designers
Lee Busch,
Richard Dickinson

Client
Continuum Healthcare Consultants Inc.
Design Firm
Sharp Designs
Designer
Stephanie Sharp

Client
Rick Kooker Photography
Design Firm
Rassman Design
Designer
John Rassman

Client
Ralph Mennemeyer
Design Firm
Hutter Design
Designer
Lea Ann Hutter

Client
HBO—U.S. Comedy Arts Festival
Design Firm
Tornado Design
Designers
Al Quattrocchi, Jeff Smith
Illustrator
Keith Weesner

Client
California DECA
Design Firm
Jiva Creative
Designer
Eric Lee

Client
Oregon Family Outings
Design Firm
Jeff Fisher LogoMotives
Designer
Jeff Fisher

Client
Swain Entertainment
Design Firm
D4 Creative Group
Designer
Wicky Lee

Client
Riding to Recovery—Lucia Livermore
Design Firm
Schum & Associates, Inc.
Designers
Guy-Franz Schum,
Ephraim Schum

Client
X Development
Design Firm
tompertdesign
Designers
Claudia Huber Tompert,
Michael Tompert

Client
Athletes In Action
Design Firm
VMA
Designers
Steven Goubeaux, Al Hidalgo

Client
Atkins Nutritionals
Design Firm
Gauger & Silva
Designer
Bob Ankers

Client
Southeast Texas Regional Airport
Design Firm
Michael Lee Advertising & Design Inc.
Designer
Michael Lee

Client
Best Doctors
Design Firm
Levine & Associates
Designers
Lena Markley, Monica Snellings

Client
NFL Films
Design Firm
Paragraph Design
Designer
Bob Aretz

Client
Nabisco
Design Firm
Stephen Longo Design Associates
Designer
Stephen Longo

Client
Kelly King & Associates
Design Firm
Funk/Levis & Associates
Designer
Alex Wijnen

Client
League to Save Lake Tahoe
Design Firm
Rosenberger Design
Designer
Shawn Rosenberger

Client
Drive Financial
Design Firm
Kendall Creative Shop
Designers
Tim Childress, Mark K. Platt

Client
The Genesis Group
Design Firm
Mindpower, Inc.
Designers
Jim McCune, Libby Turner

Client
Schiedermayer & Associates
Design Firm
Mires
Creative Director
John Ball
Designer
Miguel Perez

Client
D&R International
Design Firm
Lazarus Design
Designers
Robin Lazarus-Berlin, Jim Russell

Client
Gernot's Victoria House Restaurant
Design Firm
The Wecker Group
Designer
Robert Wecker

Client
Idea Counselors
Design Firm
Lee Busch Design
Designer
Lee Busch

Client
Sea Country Homes
Design Firm
Greenhaus
Designers
Tracy Sabin, Sandra Sharp, Craig Fuller

Client
Fog City Stables
Design Firm
Tornado Design
Designers
Al Quattrocchi,
Jeff Smith

Client
KB Greenhouses
Design Firm
Leopard
Creative Director
Brendan Hemp
Designers
Rene Larson,
Brendan Hemp

Client
Manutech
Design Firm
The Wecker Group
Designer
Robert Wecker

Client
Coast National Bank
Design Firm
Pierre Rademaker Design
Designers
Pierre Rademaker, Debbie Shibata

Client
Rene Stern/Windermere Real Estate
Design Firm
Lemley Design Company
Designers
David Lemley,
Yuri Shvets

Client
Zareba Systems
Larsen Design + Interactive
Designer
Liina Koukkari

Client
North Star Electric
Design Firm
Gage Design
Designer
Chris Roberts

Client
Dumas & McPhail
Design Firm
Pixallure Design
Designers
Steven Lutz,
Billie Green, Terry Edeker

Client
Studio No. 22
Design Firm
**Axis Design
Communications,
Inc.**
Designers
Holly T. Stein, Kelly Gillum

Client
Fringe
Design Firm
Stahl Design Inc
Designer
David Stahl

Client
University Children's Foundation
Design Firm
Liz J. Design, Inc.
Designer
Bryan Barnes

Client
Green Field Paper Company
Mires Design
Creative Director
José Serrano
Designer
Miguel Perez
Illustrator
Tracy Sabin

Client
Callery & Company
Design Firm
Callery & Company
Designer
Kelley Callery

Client
Supringo!
Design Firm
Axis Design Communications, Inc.
Designer
Holly T. Stein

Client
Iris Photographic
Design Firm
tompertdesign
Designers
Claudia Huber Tompert, Michael Tompert

Client
Robinson Knife Company
Design Firm
Michael Orr + Associates, Inc.
Designers
Michael R. Orr, Thomas Freeland

Client
The Coca-Cola Company, Inc.
Design Firm
Jones Worley Design, Inc.
Designer
Michael Sater

Client
Arts of the Southern Finger Lakes
Design Firm
Michael Orr + Associates, Inc.
Designers
Michael R. Orr,
Scott Dziura

Client
White Cloud Coffee
Design Firm
Ethos Design Group
Designer
Matthew T. White

Client
Asher Studio
Design Firm
Asher Studio
Designer
Gretchen Wills

Client
Palace Construction
Design Firm
Asher Studio
Designer
Eric Meredith

ASHER STUDIO

Client
Wirestone
Design Firm
Dula Image Group
Designer
Michael Dula

wirestone

Client
Daystar Sports
Design Firm
The Wecker Group
Designer
Robert Wecker

Client
Auction for the Arts
Design Firm
Daigle Design
Designer
Paul A. Dunning

Auction for the ART

Client
Senscom
Design Firm
Crouch and Naegeli/Design Group West
Designer
Jim Naegeli

senscom

Client
Openfirst
Design Firm
Crouch and Naegeli/Design Group West
Designer
Jim Naegeli

Openfirst

Client
North County Humane Society
Design Firm
**Winter
Advertising Agency**
Designer
Mary Winter

North County
HUMANE
SOCIETY
& S P C A

Client
Auntie Anne's
Design Firm
**McKnight
Kurland
Baccelli**

Auntie Anne's
cre amo
Classic Cones

Client
Caras & Schulman
Design Firm
Doerr Associates
Designer
Linda Blacksmith

CARAS AND SHULMAN
Certified Public Accountants

Client
Sony Computer Entertainment America
Design Firm
Creative Dynamics, Inc.
Designers
Mackenzie Walsh, Eddie Roberts,
Victor Rodriguez, Casey Corcoran

Client
Rivermark
Design Firm
Gauger & Silva
Designer
Bob Ankers

Client
Beaver County Transit Authority
Design Firm
Ideahaus®
Designer
Kevin Popovic

Client
World Golf Foundation
Design Firm
HardBall Sports
Designer
Andy Gosendi

Client
Intelsat
Design Firm
Addison
Designers
Tina Antonopoulos,
Richard Colbourne, David Kohler

Client
The Scott Deakins Company
Design Firm
Kendall Creative Shop
Designer
Mark K. Platt

Client
National Academy of Recording Arts & Sciences
Design Firm
30sixty Design, Inc.
Designers
Par Larsson, Henry Vizcarra

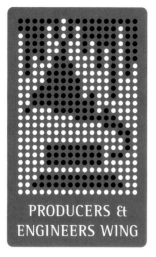

PRODUCERS &
ENGINEERS WING

Client
Waimea Smiles
Design Firm
Schnider & Yoshina Ltd.
Designer
Monica Bühlmann

Client
Kraft Foods
Design Firm
Rule29
Designer
Justin Ahrens

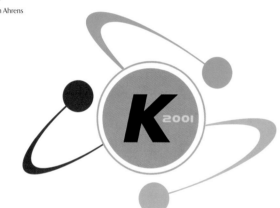

Client
Lighthouse Marketing Services, Inc.
Design Firm
Rule29
Designers
Justin Ahrens, Jim Boborci

Client
St. Martin-in-the-Field Church
Design Firm
Crowley Webb and Associates
Designer
Bonny Chruscicki

ST MARTIN-IN-THE-FIELDS
E P I S C O P A L   C H U R C H

Client
Welcome to Loudoun
Design Firm
Spot Color Incorporated
Designer
Jennifer Sterling

296

Client
Concepts In Meetings & Events
Design Firm
Sewickley Graphics & Design, Inc.
Designer
Michael Seidl

Client
Spoon
Design Firm
Bruce Yelaska Design
Designer
Bruce Yelaska

Client
Operon Group
Design Firm
Hershey Communications, Inc.
Designer
Lan Hoang Vu

Client
Drive Financial
Design Firm
Kendall Creative Shop
Designer
Tim Childress

Client
Ampure Electronics
Design Firm
Rule29
Designers
Justin Ahrens,
Jon McGrath, Jim Boborci

Client
Drive Financial
Design Firm
Kendall Creative Shop
Designer
Jennifer Brehm

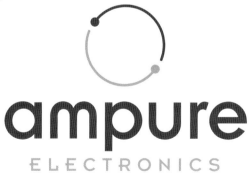

Client
Liberty Irrigation
Design Firm
Kendall Creative Shop
Designers
Jennifer Brehm,
Mark K. Platt

Client
Synchronoss
Design Firm
Gillespie
Designers
Jane Keller,
Janine Lazur

Client
The Marketing Formula
Design Firm
The Marketing Formula
Art Director, Designer
Errin Hahn

Client
Valley Printers
Design Firm
Liz J. Design, Inc.
Designer
Bryan Barnes

Client
Pittsburgh Regional Alliance
Design Firm
A to Z communications, inc.
Designer
Scott Bowlin

Client
Kalista Kollection
Design Firm
Rabil & Bates Design
Designer
Seth Sirbaugh

Client
Aionet
Design Firm
Stedman Design
Designer
Steve Stedman

Client
Mocean Graphics
Design Firm
Tornado Design
Designers
Al Quattrocchi,
Jeff Smith

Client
DC Public Libraries
Design Firm
Beth Singer Design
Designers
Chris Hoch,
Steve Trapero

Client
Datafuzion
Design Firm
Hat Trick Creative
Designers
Lance Brown, Charlie Pate

Client
Foresight Investment Solutions
Design Firm
Sean Oakes Studios
Designer
Sean Oakes

Client
Reflexion
Design Firm
Mindpower, Inc.
Designer
Debi Quilla

Client
  Meridian International Center
Design Firm
  TGD Communications, Inc.
Designers
  Rochelle Gray, Gloria Vestal

Client
  Stone Oven
Design Firm
  DuPuis
Designers
  Steven DuPuis,
  Nobuko Komine

Client
  Tracy Techau/Scout Executive/CEO
Designer
  Jennifer Hammontree-Jones

Client
  Net Beyond Communications
Design Firm
  Elias/Savion Advertising
Designers
  Ronnie Savion, Steve Baksis

Client
  Assemblies of God Church
Design Firm
  Prejean Lobue
Designers
  Kevin Prejean,
  Gary LoBue, Jr.

Client
  Cape Ann Rowing Club
  (Ocean Rowing Event)
Design Firm
  Bridge Creative Inc.
Designer
  Amanda Field

Client
  New Art Center
Design Firm
  RainCastle Communications
Designer
  Rotam Meller

Client
Parkways Foundation
Design Firm
Davis Harrison Dion
Designers
Bob Dion,
Phil Schuldt

Client
AirSea Packing Group Ltd.
Design Firm
**Schnider &
Yoshina Ltd.**
Designer
Lesley Kunikis

Client
Sention Pharmaceuticals
Design Firm
Fassino/Design
Designer
Diane Fassino

Client
Laguna Beach
Film Festival
Design Firm
**Corporate
Visuals**
Designer
Ronald Rampley

Client
Nine Sigma
Design Firm
A to Z communications, inc.
Designer
Chris Konopack

Client
Promistar Financial
Design Firm
Adam, Filippo & Associates
Designers
Martin Perez, Robert Adam

Client
Children's Legacy
Design Firm
Asher Studio
Designer
Russ Chilcoat

Client
Gball.com
Design Firm
Mires
Creative Director
Scott Mires
Designers
Cherie Wheeler, Miguel Perez

Client
Supreme Resources, Inc.
Design Firm
The Partnership, Inc.
Designer
Sim Wong

Client
Artist and Display Supply Inc.
Design Firm
Artist and Display Supply Inc.
Designer
Nora Hackenberg

Client
Sakai Village
Design Firm
Daigle Design
Designers
Candace Daigle, Gloria Chen,
Paul A. Dunning, Dan Thompson
Illustrator
Jane Shasky

Sakai Village

A RESIDENTIAL COMMUNITY ON BAINBRIDGE ISLAND

Client
Labor Management Partnership
Design Firm
Alterpop
Designer
Christopher Simmons

$(L+M)^P$

The Power of Partnership

Client
Digital Defenders
Design Firm
Grasp Creative
Designers
Doug Fuller, Aaron Taylor

DIGITAL ▨ DEFENDERS

Client
Maneval Zambito
Design Firm
Fuszion Collaborative
Designer
Steve Dreyer,
Richard Lee Heffner

MANEVAL
ZAMBITO
ARCHITECTS

Client
Washington Renegades
Design Firm
Fuszion Collaborative
Designer
Richard Lee Heffner

Client
Skil
Design Firm
Edelman Design Worldwide
Designer
Joe Ondrla

Client
West Corporation
Design Firm
Liska + Associates, Inc.

Client
Deka Design
Design Firm
Deka Design
Designer
Dmitry Krasny

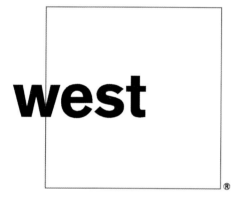

Client
Wilbur Entertainment
Design Firm
Gunion Design
Designer
Jefrey Gunion

Client
U.S. Conference of Mayors
Design Firm
Fuszion Collaborative
Designer
John Foster

Client
BK Enterprises NW
Design Firm
Jeff Fisher LogoMotives
Designer
Jeff Fisher

Client
Asset Intertech
Design Firm
RSW Creative
Creative Director
Paul Jerde
Designer
Kevin Hurley

Client
University of North Texas
Design Firm
RSW Creative
Creative Director
Paul Jerde
Designer
Audrey Thomason

Client
Black Dog Furniture Design
Design Firm
Jeff Fisher LogoMotives
Designer
Jeff Fisher
Illustrator
Brett Bigham

Client
Blackstone
Design Firm
Defteling Design
Designer
Alex Wijnen

Client
Foth & Van Dyke—Production Systems SBU
Design Firm
Foth & Van Dyke
Designer
Daniel Green

Client
Don Bonsey Photography
Design Firm
Dula Image Group
Designer
Michael Dula

Client
San Diego Historical Society
Design Firm
Crouch and Naegeli/Design Group West
Designer
Jim Naegeli

Client
Credant Technologies
Design Firm
RSW Creative
Creative Director
Paul Jerde
Designer
Kevin Hurley

Client
Serbian National Federation
Design Firm
Ideahaus®
Designer
Kevin Popovic

Client
Cooper & Associates
Design Firm
Jeff Fisher LogoMotives
Designer
Jeff Fisher

Client
Creative Culinary Design
Design Firm
Dula Image Group
Designer
Michael Dula

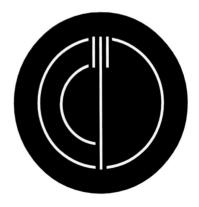

Client
City Parks
Design Firm
A to Z communications, inc.
Designer
Ilena Finocchi

Client
First National Bank of Omaha
Design Firm
Sacco Group
Designers
Scott Bargenquast, Jeff Walker

Client
Cibo Naturals
Design Firm
Daigle Design
Designer
Candace Daigle

Client
UO Housing (University of Oregon)
Design Firm
Funk/Levis & Associates
Designer
Beverly Soasey

Client
Low Fruit Search
Design Firm
Mindpower, Inc.
Designer
Niki Walker

Client
Grassroot Institute of Hawaii
Design Firm
Genghis Design
Designers
Dale Monahan, David Tisdale

Client
Torrefazione Italia
Design Firm
Phinney Bischoff Design House
Designers
Dean Hart, Brian Buckner

Client
Freshkist Produce, LLC
Design Firm
CRG
Designer
Rory Vance

Client
Epicurean Kitchens of Sewickley
Design Firm
Sewickley Graphics & Design, Inc.
Designer
Jim Reybein

Client
Green Mountain College
Design Firm
Mindpower, Inc.
Designer
Niki Walker

Client
Heda Property Management
Design Firm
The Partnership, Inc.
Designer
Sim Wong

Client
Vans Salon
Design Firm
Ideahaus®
Designer
Kevin Popovic

(leaf change is made the
first day of the season, i.e.
yellow=spring,
green=summer,
orange=fall,
blue=winter)

Client
Stone Network–Shelly Barnum
Design Firm
Ripple Strategic Design & Consulting
Designer
Raymond Perez

Client
Panda Restaurant Group
Design Firm
Mike Salisbury, L.L.C.
Designers
Mike Salisbury, Dick Sakahara, Travis Page

Client
David Lessnick
Design Firm
Creative Dynamics, Inc.
Designer
Victor Rodriguez

Client
DiviDivi
Design Firm
Mike Salisbury, L.L.C.

Client
Sleep Over Bagzzz
Design Firm
Davies Associates
Designers
Cathy Davies,
John Andrew Padrutt

Client
Physio Arts
Design Firm
Berkeley Design L.L.C.
Designer
Larry Torno

Client
SAFECO
Design Firm
Phinney Bischoff Design House
Designers
Cody Rasmussen, Leslie Phinney

Client
Pain Management Institute
Design Firm
Fritz Creative
Designers
Kathy Fritz,
Jenny Van Setters

Client
Toys 'R' Us
Design Firm
Shea
Designer
Jason Wittwer

Client
Robert Wood Johnson Foundation
Design Firm
Graves Fowler Associates
Designer
Victoria Q Robinson

Client
Saint Louis Zoo
Design Firm
Bright Rain Creative
Designer, Illustrator
Matt Marino

Active for Life

Client
Woodland Lakes
Design Firm
Hunter Advertising
Designer
Carolyn J. Hunter

Client
Tierra
Design Firm
Crouch and Naegeli/Design Group West
Designer
Amy Gingery

Client
Aloha Restaurants, Inc.
Design Firm
Dula Image Group
Designer
Michael Dula

Client
Maxim Home Loan, Inc.
Design Firm
The Partnership, Inc.
Designer
Sim Wong

HOME LOAN

Client
MarketJazz
Design Firm
Crouch and Naegeli/Design Group West
Designer
Jim Naegeli

Client
Festival of the Family
Design Firm
Creghead & Harrold Inc.
Designer
Stacie Ormerod

Client
Exhibit A
Design Firm
Kendall Creative Shop
Designers
Tim Childress, Mark K. Platt

Client
Intessa
Design Firm
Gauger & Silva
Designer
Rob Keil

Client
Shea Homes
Design Firm
Gauger & Silva
Designer
Lori Murphy

Client
QSR Concepts, Inc.
Design Firm
Dula Image Group
Designer
Michael Dula

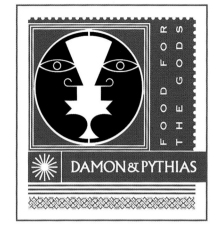

Client
Abel/Noser
Design Firm
Cullinane Design
Designer
Carmen Li

trade-zoom™

Client
Cliq Photolab
Design Firm
The Partnership, Inc.
Designer
Sim Wong

Client
JNR Incorporated
Design Firm
Laura Coe Design Assoc.
Designer
Ryoichi Yotsumoto

Client
GrandSlam Transportation Inc.
Design Firm
Never Boring Design
Designer
Melody MacMurray

Birds of Two Worlds

SYMPOSIUM 2002

INDEX

DESIGN FIRMS

CLIENTS